SHEM'ON THE GRACEFUL

DISCOURSE ON THE SOLITARY LIFE

Translation and Introduction by
Mary Hansbury

Preface by

Sebastian Brock

SLG Press
Convent of the Incarnation
Fairacres, Parker Street
Oxford OX4 1TB
www.slgpress.co.uk

Fairacres Publications No. 184

Print ISBN 978-0-7283-0301-0
ISSN 0307-1405

Edited and typeset in Palatino by Julia Craig-McFeely

The cover picture is a detail from Tuscan, *c.* 1440–1450, *Scenes from the lives of the Hermits: St Benedict, Abba Macarius and others*, JBS 21 reproduced from the original painting in the Picture Gallery of Christ Church, Oxford by kind permission of the Governing Body of Christ Church, Oxford.

SLG Press
Convent of the Incarnation
Fairacres Oxford
www.slgpress.co.uk
Printed by
Grosvenor Group Ltd, Loughton, Essex

CONTENTS

PREFACE

Shem`on d-Taibutheh, or Symeon 'of the Book of Grace', is unlikely to be a name familiar to many readers. Shem`on is, however, one of a number of quite remarkable monastic writers of the late seventh century produced by the Church of the East, the best-known of these authors being St Isaac the Syrian, or St Isaac of Nineveh. A near contemporary of Bede but living at the other end of the Christian world, and already under Arab rule, Symeon must have had a medical training, evident from the selection of his monastic writings translated into English by Alphonse Mingana in his important series, somewhat misleadingly entitled 'Early Christian Mystics'.[1] Virtually the only other thing known about Symeon is the fact that he became a hermit attached to a famous monastery known under the name of an earlier monastic Abba, Rabban Shabur. Although the exact location of this monastery is unknown, it must have been situated somewhere in the mountainous region of south-west Iran.

In recent decades it was Paolo Bettiolo who first drew attention to the interest of Symeon's writings in his *Simone di Taibuteh. Violenza e grazia: la coltura del cuoro*, in the course of which he provided an Italian translation, based on manuscripts, of the work which is translated here. The Syriac original is only now about to see the light of day, but its potential interest for modern readers had also been indicated by the late Father André Louf in his French translation of 2002, published in Volume 64 of *Collectanea Cisterciensia*.[2] As the title of the work suggests, the Discourse, or Homily, is addressed to an experienced monk who is about to adopt the life of a solitary, and it will have been given on the occasion of the consecration of his cell. In it Symeon emphasises the momentous nature of the undertaking and

---

[1] Mingana, *Shem`on the Graceful, Medico-Mystical Work*.
[2] Louf, 'Discours sur la cellule'.

warns the solitary of the need to be fully aware of the difficulties and spiritual dangers that his new life will involve in the ascetic struggle of trying to live a life of stillness (Greek *hesychia*, Syriac *shelya*) and to become (in St Bruno's words) *Christo quietus*, 'still in and for Christ'. It so happens that a third monk associated with the Monastery of Rabban Shabur, Dadisho', was the author of a treatise specifically devoted to the topic of *shelya*, parts of which were included in Mingana's Early Christian Mystics.

Symeon's other main work, entitled *The Book of Grace* (after which he is often named), is in the form of short sections on a great variety of aspects of the spiritual life. Although the full text has not yet been published, an English translation of extensive extracts can be found in an Appendix to the first edition only (1984) of the Holy Transfiguration Monastery's translation of *The Ascetical Homilies of Saint Isaac the Syrian*, where, following a number of the manuscripts, the work is attributed to St Isaac, an attribution now considered not so likely.[3]

English readers will be most grateful to the translator, Dr Mary Hansbury, for making Symeon's 'Discourse on the Consecration of the Cell' available to a modern readership. Mary Hansbury is an experienced translator of Syriac monastic texts; among those that she has published in recent years are *The Dialogue on the Soul* by the fifth-century author John the Solitary (also known as John of Apamea), and the recently discovered 'Third Collection' of Discourses by St Isaac the Syrian.[4]

Sebastian Brock
Oriental Institute, Oxford, 2019

---

[3] Miller, 'Selections from the Book of Grace'.

[4] Hansbury, *John the Solitary on the Soul* and Hansbury, *Isaac the Syrian's Spiritual Works (III, V)*.

SHEM`ON THE GRACEFUL

SHEM`ON THE GRACEFUL

Shem`on the Graceful was a Syriac monk in the seventh century. He may be best understood in the context of the solitary life. *Iḥîdâyâ* refers to the soul alone with God and is a key term in East Syrian writers of the seventh and eighth centuries. As early as St Ephrem (d. 373) *îḥîdâyâ* means 'solitary', living a solitary life rather than in a monastery (*dâyrâyâ*). It is a form of consecrated life within the community. *Iḥîdâyâ* has the following connotations: *îḥîdâ* (noun) and *îḥîdâyâ* (adj.) may refer to Christ, the Only-Begotten (John 1:14; 3:10); applied to the Christian life, *îḥîdâyâ* has the sense of unique, singular, single as in celibate, single-minded, unified, follower of Christ. In the early church baptism came later in life, as an adult; at baptism ascetic vows might be taken to live as a solitary. Solitaries could live within their family and could help within the community, as did St Ephrem, or retire for prayer. Sebastian Brock notes the resonances of the terms with Jewish Targumim where *îḥîdâ* is used referring both to God and to Adam—representing humanity—in the pre-Fall state.[1] In Shem`on's teaching, the life of the inner person is in a state of spiritual growth, striving to return to the pre-Fall status of Adam and so become an imitator of Christ the *Iḥîdâ*.

Shem`on's name of Taibutheh, 'the Graceful', is thought to have been given because of his insistence on the role of divine grace in salvation history.

---

[1] See Brock, 'The Syriac Orient: A Third "Lung" for the Church?', 5–20; Brock, *The Luminous Eye: The Spiritual World Vision of St. Ephrem,* 133–41; Brock, *Spirituality in the Syriac Tradition,* 49–59. S. Griffith comments at length on the thinking of Aphrahat (early 4th c.) on *îḥîdâyâ* in the Demonstrations in his '"Singles" in God's Service; Thoughts on the Ihidaye from the Works of Aphrahat and Ephraem the Syrian'.

… it is through the Economy of His grace that He released us from the swaddling clothes of the tangible darkness of the bodily covering of substances and natures, and brought us to the intelligible knowledge of the theory of the spiritual powers, which is hidden and works in everything …[2]

Shem`on seems to have been a doctor before becoming a monk. He lived under the Patriarch Henanisho in eastern Syria and died *c.*680. His writings available in translation include:

— Writings on the spiritual life, often referred to as a Medico-Mystical work, perhaps because of Shem`on's detailed medical imagery.[3]

— A discourse on the consecration of the cell.[4]

— Writings referred to as *The Book of Grace,* originally attributed to Isaac the Syrian, now recognized as the work of Shem`on.[5]

The focus of this study is the discourse on the consecration of the cell.[6] The notes to the translation include illustrations from others of the 'golden age of Syriac Christian literature,' an expression used by Hilarion Alfeyev to describe seventh- and eighth-century Syriac writers. He lists Sahdona, Dadisho', Isaac, Shem`on, John of Daly-atha, and Joseph Hazzaya.[7] Perhaps the intensity of their mystical language (and lack of Christological concerns) is not surprising in that each had a personal experience of solitary life.

Sahdona (7th c.) was born near Kirkuk, in modern-day Iraq. He was bishop of Beth Garmai. After being deposed for doc-

---

[2] Mingana, trans., *Shem`on the Graceful, Medico-Mystical Work,* 12.

[3] ibid. 1–69 which includes both Syriac and English texts.

[4] ibid. See also Bettiolo, *Simone di Taibuteh. Violenza e grazia: la coltura del cuore;* Chialà, *Abitare la solitudine;* Louf, 'Discours sur la cellule'.

[5] Partial translation, Miller 'Selections from the Book of Grace'. Partial unpublished translation by A. Louf. Translation in progress by Grigory Kessel.

[6] The translation of this discourse was made from a copy of a manuscript in the Biblioteca Apostolica Vaticana: Vat.sir.509, folios 50v–61v. The manuscript was transcribed and edited by Rahmani in 1928; Sabino Chialà of the Monastery of Bose kindly provided me with a copy of the Syriac text.

[7] See Alfeyev, *The Spiritual World of St Isaac,* 23.

trinal issues, he lived as a solitary near Edessa. He wrote
two treatises on the solitary life as well as five letters.[8]

Dadisho' (7th c.) was a contemporary of Isaac. Both were from
Qatar. The introduction to his *Discourse on Solitude* describes
Dadisho as a solitary and spiritual philosopher.[9]

John of Dalyatha (8th c.) was born in Iraq; after seven years as a
monk near the Turkish border he became a solitary in the moun-
tains of Dalyatha. In his *Letters* he speaks about God in human
language as perhaps no other Christian author has done.[10]

Joseph Hazzaya (8th c.) was born Zoroastrian; taken captive he
was sold to a Christian in north Iraq. As a monk he lived the
solitary life for two periods and was also abbot of Mar Bassima
and Rabban Bokhtisho.[11]

Isaac, known as the Syrian or Isaac of Nineveh (7th c.), was born
in eastern Arabia; he entered a monastery and after many
years of study became involved in religious education
throughout the Beth Qatraye region. After a short time as
Bishop of Nineveh he went to the wilderness of Mount Matout
where he spent many years in solitude and fasting. He is best
remembered for his writings on Christian asceticism.[12]

---

[8] See de Halleux, *Martyrius (Sahdona), Oeuvres spirituelles. I–III. Livre de la perfection; IV. Lettres à des amis solitaire, maximes sapientales.*

[9] Mingana, *Shem`on the Graceful, Medico-Mystical Work*; Mingana, *Treatise on Solitude and Prayer: on Seven Weeks of Solitude.*

[10] Beulay, *La collection des Lettres de Jean de Dalyatha*; Hansbury, *The Letters of John of Dalyatha*; Khayat, *Jean de Dalyatha, les Homélies I–XV.*

[11] Albert, *Joseph Ḥazzayâ. Lettre sur les trois étapes de la vie monastique*; Lazzeri, *Giuseppe Hazzaya. Le tappe della vita spirituale.*

[12] For **Isaac I** see Wensinck, *Mystic Treatises by Isaac of Nineveh*. For **Isaac II** see Brock, *Isaac of Nineveh (Isaac the Syrian). 'The Second Part', Chapters IV-XLI*; Bettiolo, *Isacco di Ninive. Discorsi spirituali: capitoli sulla conoscenza, preghiere, contemplazione sull'argomento della gehenna, altri opuscoli.* For **Isaac III** see Chialà, *Isacco di Ninive. Terza collezione*; Hansbury, *Isaac the Syrian's Spiritual Works (III, V)*; Louf, *Isaac le Syrien. Œuvres spirituelles II. Discours récemment découverts*; Louf, *Isaac le Syrien. Œuvres spirituelles III. D'après un manuscrit récemment.* For *Discorsi spirituali* see **Isaac II**.

The bulk of my comments come from Isaac, very close in time to Shem`on, and arguably the richest of Syriac mystical writers, but I have also included comments from Evagrius (d. 399), Macarius (4th c.) and John the Solitary (5th c.), earlier writers who were thought to have influenced Shem`on.[13]

There is a predilection for medical imagery in the early Syriac authors;[14] it remains to be seen whether or not this influence can be traced to Nemesius of Emesa (late 4th c.) given the earlier dating of his *On the Nature of Man* (c. 390) as noted by Zonta.[15] Shem`on includes detailed medical imagery in his writings: in his *Book of Medicine* (translated by Mingana) a strikingly detailed anatomical discussion is found.[16] Medical imagery is found as early as Ephrem, whose *Hymn of Paradise V* may be at the root of this thinking. Shemunkasho makes an important distinction about healing imagery being based on Nature, that is Ephrem's 'Book of Nature' and not natural theology as a philosophical investigation. Rather, the basis of his contemplation is the 'two books' of Nature and Scripture mentioned in the *Hymn of Paradise V*.[17]

> In his book Moses
> described the creation of the natural world,
> so that both Nature and Scripture

---

[13] For **Evagrius** see Bamberger, *Evagrius Ponticus. The Prakticos & Chapters on Prayer*; Guillaumont, *Évagre le Pontique, Les six centuries des 'Kephalaia Gnostica'*. *The Ascetical Homilies of Saint Isaac the Syrian*. For **John the Solitary** see Hansbury, *John the Solitary on the Soul*; Lavenant, *Jean d'Apamée. Dialogues et traités*.

[14] See Blum, 'The Mystology of John the Solitary from Apamea', 114. See Hansbury, *John the Solitary on the Soul*, 4th Discourse 82–4 for his extensive use of medical terminolgy.

[15] Zonta, 'Nemesiana Syriaca: New Fragments from the Missing Syriac Version of the *De Natura Hominis*'.

[16] Mingana, *Treatise on Solitude and Prayer: On Seven Weeks of Solitude*, 62–3. Kessel addresses the issue of medical imagery in relation to this work in 'La position de Simon de Taibuteh dans l'éventail de la tradition mystique syriaque', 142–6, which includes a discussion of Aḥûdemmêh (d. 575).

[17] Shemunkasho, *Healing in the Theology of Saint Ephrem*, see Ch. 5, 'Salvation History as a Process of Healing'.

might bear witness to the Creator:
Nature through man's use of it,
Scripture, through his reading of it.[18]

Brock says medical imagery in Ephrem merits further study because it permeates the writings of other early Syriac writers.[19] Shemunkasho has noted seventy references to Jesus in the New Testament as the one who heals, and in Ephrem he shows the usage of the term *âsyâ*/physician for Jesus: the heavenly Physician, the wise Physician, the great Physician, the good Physician, the pure Physician.[20]

I have included some bibliography for Jacob of Serug. Sidney Griffith points to Evagrian 'thought and language' in Jacob, perhaps by way of Philoxenus, and suggests Jacob as a bridge between earlier Syriac patterns of mysticism and the 'golden age' of the seventh and eighth centuries, referred to by Alfeyev.[21]

One of the most significant aspects of the present treatise is how Shem'on speaks of entering into the cell and persevering inside oneself, within the inner being.[22] The purpose of dwelling in the cell is to discover the existence of an interior person or dimension within the exterior one. Death from the world prepares an inner world where God reveals Himself and the Spirit celebrates liturgy on the altar of the heart. The solitary must try to enter this place, and in doing so

---

[18] See Brock in *Ephrem the Syrian, Hymns on Paradise*, 102 and 'Humanity and the Natural World'.

[19] See Brock, *The Luminous Eye: The Spiritual World Vision of St. Ephrem*, 40.

[20] See Shemunkasho, *Healing in the Theology of Saint Ephrem*, 119–40; and see 412–13 (with quotes from Ephrem): 'Jesus' healing ability symbolizes that He is the Son of the Creator, for healing is something divine, and it can be called a "second creation". As God created the world, Jesus fulfilled it by His healing'.

[21] See Griffith, 'Mar Jacob of Serugh on Monks and Monasticism: Readings in his Metrical Homilies "On the singles"' and his extended study, *Mar Jacob of Serugh on Monks and Monasticism. Readings in his Metrical Homilies 'On the Singles'*, 84, where he quotes from Reed and Scott, *Jacob of Sarug's Homilies on the Solitaries*.

[22] Cf. Rom. 7:22; Eph. 3:16. See also McCollum, *Jacob of Sarug's Homilies on Jesus' Temptation*.

teaches others how to live interiority prophetically. Prophecy is not just predicting, telling the future, but is revealing God's will and interpreting it in the present, not as a metaphor but in a symbolic way. Of course this does have a future dimension in that it is the life after the resurrection, founded in hope and established in baptism, that is revealed in the solitary as he dwells in stillness. Perhaps Shem`on is also saying that not only does the solitary make the resurrected life known but he helps to actualize it by the conduct of the inner person. 'If after baptism one remains in a state of spiritual growth, one is already in the new life of the new world.'[23] The solitary alerts others to a dimension of life which can only be perceived in solitude but which is the new creation in the inner world of all Christians.[24]

---

[23] Isaac II v.5.

[24] Both John the Solitary and John of Dalyatha also lived the solitary life as an anticipation of the resurrected life, but in Shem`on it seems even more explicit. See the comments of Chialà in 'Simone di Taibuteh e il suo insegnamento sulla vita nella cella', 136–8.

DISCOURSE ON THE SOLITARY LIFE

*Again a profitable discourse spoken on the day of
the consecration of the cell, when a brother goes out
from the cenobium, composed by the holy Mar
Shem`on the Graceful, called Luke,
disciple of Rabban Shabur the Huzita.*

1 O blessed brothers, friends of Christ, we are invited today to
the spiritual marriage feast of this our brother who has separated himself to sit in the cell. From evening until morning we
have invoked God for him, by a vigil and the Office, by prayers
and hymns of the Spirit. Even now we make supplication to our
Lord the Christ, by the prayer of his saints, to strengthen, protect,
renew and sanctify the perfection of his will in the likeness of the
holy Fathers who have become well known in the way of quiet in
the cell, forever. Amen

2 We have learned and received from our glorious Fathers who
have persevered within the solitary life and have endured violent battles, afflictions, temptations of nature or of the demons.
They have become renowned in the struggle against the passions
and desires; and with divine aid have preserved their life in the harbour of purity and limpidity.[25] They received a double crown[26] at

---

[25] According to Beulay, one enters the spiritual order when purity (*dakyûṯâ*)
is attained. The more positive aspect of this is limpidity (*šapyûṯâ*) which
gives perception of the new world. Beulay discusses this in the context of
John the Solitary. See Beulay, *La lumière sans forme. Introduction a l'étude de
la mystique chrétienne syro-orientale*, 100. Limpidity of soul occurs often in
John the Solitary. See Hansbury, *John the Solitary on the Soul*. See also
de Halleux, *Martyrius [Sahdona] Œuvres spirituelles*, I, 17, 56; Isaac I LXVII;
Draguet, *Commentaire du livre d'Abba Isaïe par Dadiso Qatraya* IV.5. For references to limpidity of mind see Isaac II XXI.7. John the Solitary says that
Christ is the model for limpidity, see Lavenant, *Jean d'Apamée. Dialogues et
traités*, 42–3, IX.96. And Jacob of Serug calls Christ 'the Luminous One', in
his Homily on the Presentation, line 310, see Kollamparampil, *Jacob of
Serugh, Select Festal Homilies*, 154.

[26] Cf. 2 Tim. 4:7–8.

the completion of the course of their struggles. So now we propose also to this our brother a few admonitions useful for sitting in the cell, that one might conduct one's spiritual life according to them.

3 First of all, then, O brother capable of discernment who have separated yourself to sit in the cell, we make known to your divine charity that you consecrate today not only the cell with hymns, praises and canticles of the Holy Spirit, but it is you yourself that you separate and offer *to God as a living sacrifice.*[27] It happens as with ordinary vessels which, as soon as they have been separated and consecrated in the Spirit, become completely different: consecrated to the Lord[28] with a double honour by means of the descent[29] of the Holy Spirit. Also you, our brother, who separated yourself today and have consecrated and offered yourself to God through prayers, praise and hymns of the Spirit, you are henceforth holy to the Lord in the sanctification of your body and to God in the splendour of your soul, in the newness of a divine way of life which will be visible in you day after day as you draw near to God. So from today you place a different foundation to your life, your way of life and your divine manner of life, on which your soul with your body may be renewed and sanctified by the Spirit in the Office and in the prayers, hymns and canticles of the Holy Spirit, that in your cell you will continually offer to Christ who has chosen you and drawn you from the world and brought you to this angelic way of life. Even the holy angels desire to continue singing the hymns unceasingly, which in ways both hidden and open, you offer to God in your cell at all times.

---

[27] Cf. Rom. 12:1.

[28] Ex. 30:37.

[29] Descent (*rûḥâfâ*) from the verb *rḥf* as found in Gen. 1:2. In his 'Commentary on Genesis' Ephrem discusses how it is seen by some as an 'activity of creation'; see Mathews and Amar, *Saint Ephrem the Syrian, Selected Prose Works*, 76–9. John the Solitary links *ruḥâfâ* with baptism saying that it is not the nature of the waters that renews us but the 'hidden power', *ruḥâfâ d-ḥaylâ kasyâ*, see Hansbury, *John the Solitary on the Soul*, 184. See also the comments of Bettiolo, *Simone di Taibuteh. Violenza e grazia: la coltura del cuore*, 136–7.

4 Therefore you ought to cut off entirely the former habits of your upbringing which you practiced in the cenobium in the midst of your blessed brothers, so that from this time forward you might become completely light and salt of the Gospel, as our Lord says,[30] for yourself and for all your acquaintances. However, I make known to your divine charity that if you do not cut off your former habits and do not renew yourself in the Spirit and do not forcefully guard your sight and your hearing, nor curb your tongue with silence, and when you go outside from your cell, whether for church or for any affair, but do not carefully guard your gaze and your tongue until you are accustomed to the silence, your labour in your cell will be unprofitable.

And if you do not persevere in your cell, like a hen sitting on its young until the cell have mercy on you and draw you to itself, grace will not rest upon you[31] and the fruits of the Spirit[32] and of divine love will not flourish in you.

And if your heart is not broken by remorse for your transgressions you will not acquire humility.

And if your body is not weakened by fasting and night vigils, the Office and prayers, prostrations and sleeping on the ground, your soul will not have the strength to resist in the struggle against the passions and desires.

And if you do not control your natural inclination and your belly and do not accustom yourself to patience in afflictions, poverty and indigence, separation from your acquaintances, the lack of life's necessities, the power of the Holy Spirit will not manifest its action in

---

[30] Matt. 5:13–14.

[31] Rest upon: *maggnânûtâ* and its root *aggen* are used to describe the descent of the Holy Spirit on the Virgin Mary (Luke 1:35) and on the gifts during the Eucharistic epiclesis. In some later monastic writings, the verb as seen here is used to indicate the activity of the Holy Spirit upon the heart during prayer, revealing the scriptural and sacramental dimensions of a life of prayer. Isaac dedicates a chapter to this, see Isaac II XVI. See also Brock, 'Maggnânûtâ: a Technical Term in East Syrian Spirituality and its Background'.

[32] Gal. 5:22.

you. And without divine strength you will not be able to endure the violence of temptations and the indignities and attack from the Evil One[33] and his hosts.

And if contempt and wrongdoing from others do not insult your innocence, the fear of God will not abide in you.

And if you do not cultivate and practice works of repentance and self-denial, you will not be able to keep the commandments of our Lord.

And if together with the labours of repentance[34] you do not keep the commandments of our Lord in fear and with love, you are not a friend of Christ.[35] Pretending to live the life in the cell, you will cultivate the passions of your desire and the demons will easily deceive you with opinions, vain glory and with various and numerous passions. Your labour will be without profit. It is written: 'The one who toils without advice, toils in vain'.[36]

---

[33] There are more than twenty mentions of the Evil One, Satan, the adversary, demons, enemies, in this discourse. One could read with profit McCollum, *Jacob of Sarug's Homilies on Jesus' Temptation*; they contain many verses on what the Evil One actually thinks and speaks.

[34] Repentance (*tyâbûtâ*), see Beulay, *L'enseignement spirituel de Jean de Dalyatha, mystique syro-oriental du VIIIe siècle*, 55–60. See John of Dalyatha's Letter 43, his longest letter, in Beulay, *La collection des lettres de Jean de Dalyatha*, 192–209. Isaac speaks of repentance as a medicine to strengthen and renew in the pursuit of righteousness, Isaac II XL.8. In Jewish midrashic material, some beautiful passages can be found on repentance. It is considered to be one of the seven things created before the creation of the world, 'The Power of Repentance' in Friedlander, *Pirke de Rabbi Eliezer: The Chapters of Rabbi Eliezer the Great*, 337–44. (this is a ninth century redaction, most of the material belonging to an earlier period). See also Urbach, *The Sages: Their Concepts and Beliefs*, 462–71. Scholem quotes a Babylonian Gaon (8th c.) linking the path of repentance with the 'ecstatic progress through the seven heavens' leading to the throne of glory, *Major Trends in Jewish Mysticism*, 78. Several scholars (P. Alexander, A. Becker, S. Brock, A. Golitzin, T. Kronholm and N. Sed) have in fact noted the presence of Jewish materials among the writings of the East Syriac tradition.

[35] Cf. John 15:14.

[36] Cf. Ps. 127.

5 You, then, our beloved, at the beginning of every aspect of life in your cell, acquire for yourself goodness of soul which is the likeness of God. As it is written: whoever's eye is pure does not see evil.[37] You then acquire for yourself a good eye which does not envy and does not see the weaknesses of others and does not judge the neighbour. Acquire tranquillity, humility, humiliation, patience in affliction and a simple faith; sincere love towards all,[38] hope in God, pleasing ways, firm habits, a peaceful manner of life without litigating; obedience, hard labour, diligence in all work.

6 Cut off memories, good and bad, of friends as well as of enemies. Do not think of anyone near or far. Let the remembrance[39] of our Lord and his graces to you be never ceasing in your heart: how He snatched you from your companions and from the mire of the world and brought you to this way of holiness. And behold, you dwell in the midst of saints, *children of light*.[40] Instead of the buying and selling carried on freely in the world, fill your

---

[37] Cf. Hab. 1:13; Titus 1:15.

[38] 'Sincere love towards all': Chialà looks at the dangers of life in the cell according to Shem`on, including lack of love for others. Shem`on says that scorn for others is the most insidious temptation of solitary life. See Chialà, 'Simeone di Taibuteh e il suo insegnamento sulla vita nella cella', 129–30. Isaac saw perfection in terms of love and compassion: 'And so all the saints have reached this accomplishment when they became perfect, so that they resembled God in effusion of love and compassion for mankind. And they asked for themselves as a token of their resembling God, that they should be perfect in the love of their fellows. So did also the solitary Fathers, that they might bear in themselves constantly this likeness full of the love of Christ, the Lord of the universe.' See Isaac I LXXIV (Bedjan, 510). See also Beulay, 'L'amour mystique du prochain chez les Syro-Orientaux'. He cites examples of various authors on the aspect of mystical love, when one does not see evil in others.

[39] Remembrance of God (*'uhdânâ d-alâhâ*) is found frequently in Isaac the Syrian. Since the Incarnation occurrs not because of sin, but only because God loves mankind (*Discorsi spirituali* IV.LXXVIII) this leaves little alternative but to remember God always. This memory is kept alive by the reading (*qeryânâ*) of Scripture. See Isaac II XXX.4. And see Hansbury 'Remembrance of God and its Relation to Scripture in Isaac III, including Insights from Islamic and Jewish Traditions'.

[40] Eph. 5:8; 1 Thess. 5:5.

mouth with praise, psalms, and spiritual canticles. May your heart always be ardent to complete the seven appointed canonical hours laid down by the Fathers in the Holy Spirit for recitation in your cell, with prayers, genuflections, prostrations, petitions, tears,[41] a broken heart and weeping for your sins.

7 Do not despair at all, as if your previous sins are not forgiven. The Lord is near to the broken-hearted and He helps and saves those who call to Him with all their heart.

Do not rely at all on your labours and your self-denial, or your keeping vigil and your fasting, as if these would prepare for you *crowns of righteousness*[42] without the help, hidden and revealed, of Christ our Lord. That mouth which does not deceive has decreed: 'Without Me you can do nothing'.[43]

The labours of repentance are indeed habitations along the ways where our Fathers in the Spirit walked on that narrow path which leads to life.[44] Any solitary who, without the labours of repentance commanded by the Fathers, walks in this path of holiness in a relaxed and dissolute manner—led by error or ignorance—his end will be perdition and he prepares for himself a place in Gehenna.

8 But you, our brother, engrave in your heart the commandments of the Lord. Write them and suspend them ['as an emblem'] between your eyes[45] and meditate on them constantly. They will bring you to immutable truth.

Be careful not to accustom your tongue to vanity or excessive speech, even if it be useful, nor to falsehood or oaths or feigned arguments.

---

[41] In Isaac tears (*dem'ê*) accompany purification and rebirth; the eyes are the baptismal font, Isaac I xvii (Bedjan, 139). See Chialà, *Dall' ascesi eremitica alla misericordia infinita. Ricerche su Isacco di Ninive e la sua fortuna*, 211–13.

[42] 2 Tim. 4:8.

[43] John 15:5.

[44] Matt. 7:14.

[45] Deut. 6:6–9.

Drive away from you impure gains and love of conquering, love of honour and bodily rest.

Do not disparage anyone as evil [to his] face or in [your] heart. And [even] in your mind, do not grumble about anyone.

Be diligent with your Office, with your prayers and in the Hours assigned in your cell, and in all your manual work. Do not leave space for *acedia*,[46] laziness or negligence, lest they dominate you.

Prefer being occupied with the Office, prayer and supplications, more than converse with persons, and the Spirit of God will find a place in you. He Himself will encourage you in every good deed.

Persevere in the reading of the books of the solitary Fathers and neither *acedia* nor laziness will take possession of you. For the reading of [their] books—joined with the Office, prayer and intercession—gives light to the mind, consoles the heart and awakens the soul to the work of repentance.

Whenever possible humble yourself as inferior, wretched and the last of all the community. Ask God with sighs to guard your ways and to place the bridle of silence on your tongue. It is written: 'By your words you will be justified and by your words you will be condemned.'[47] Again it is written: 'Nothing is comparable to a small mouth for what goes in and out'.[48]

---

[46] *Acedia* (*quṭṭâpâ*): listlessness, depression. See how Jacob of Serug describes it in Scott and Reed, *Jacob of Sarug's Homilies on the Solitaries*, 92:

> By all means, the Evil One is anxious to overcome you … When a solitary takes up a book to read, he brings on listlessness and sleep and puts an end to it. Immediately when depression enters the mind, [the solitary] abandons reading and takes up counting all the pages. He saw the many pages which were in the book and became despondent. And he began to count and consider when he might finish them. Immediately he began to yawn because of his listlessness. And the [Evil One] brings him to that sleep, which comes at his command; brings sleep and hangs it above his eyes, so that by it, they might become heavy and send forth a heavy sleep upon him. As with chains, he binds a person with listlessness. And he makes [the solitaries] cease from the practice of righteousness.

[47] Matt. 12:37.

[48] Cf. James 3:10.

9 You then, our beloved, prefer more than any other virtue to bear insult and humiliations, because labours deprived of humiliations generate pride and darken the soul with opinions.[49] However, the humiliations which the solitary knowingly endures generate repentance in the soul; give light to the mind and guard one's labours. These labours generate in us the humility[50] of the followers of our Lord, which is the door of the new life.[51]

Wherever you dwell, try not to be thought much of by others but rather as the least and the last of everyone. And when our Lord has seen how you toil and constrain yourself and bow down to bear insult and humiliation, even from those who are the least and weakest, He will have mercy on you and will save you from an attack of the demons, and from the captivity of disgraceful passions.

10 I beseech you not to neglect fasting, night vigil, the Office, prayer, reading,[52] the seven Hours appointed [for recitation] in your cell lest the Evil One ravage you with his devices.

And of the things which happen to you in your cell from the Evil One who troubles you with deceit by means of *acedia*, sloth, fear, agitation, temptations and humiliations; or if grace assists you and you

---

[49] Syr. *masbrânûtâ*: opinions, suspicions, doubts.

[50] Humility (*makkîkûtâ*): Chialà looks at humility in Isaac and how it leads to divinization, 'L'umiltà nel pensiero di Isacco di Ninive: via di umanizzazione e di divinizzazione', 105–20. And see Isaac I LXXXII (Bedjan, 574):

> For humility is the garment of divinity; for the word which became man, put it on and spoke in it with us, through our body. And everyone who puts it on in truth, by humility takes the likeness of Him that has descended from His height and concealed the splendor of His majesty and hidden His glory, lest the creation should perish by the sight of Him.

[51] New life (*hayyê hadtê*): derives from Peshitta Rom. 6:4. The term is characteristic of John the Solitary, see Hansbury, *John the Solitary on the Soul*, 10, 56, 62, 91. See also Theodore of Mopsuestia, Mingana, *Commentary of Theodore of Mopsuestia on the Nicene Creed*, 12, 174–5, 183–4, 187. J. Lera traces the root of New Life in John the Solitary back to Theodore, see Lera, 'Theodore of Mopsuestia'. In de Halleux, trans., *Martyrius [Sahdona] Œuvres spirituelles, I*, 107, stillness (*šelyâ*) is considered to be an image of the New Life after the resurrection.

[52] Reading (*qeryânâ*).

receive help sometimes of joy,[53] mental rest or hidden consolation, etc., do not turn foolishly to tell others of the mercy conveyed. [Tell] only your spiritual Father and this with great prudence. It is written: 'Reveal your thoughts to your Fathers but not to just anyone'. Nor reveal to anyone the measure of your Office or how you toil, keep vigil, pray and lead a life of abstinence in your cell. Otherwise grace will forsake you[54] and you will fall into the hands of the demons who will threaten you and lay claim to you with God.

11 I beseech you: force yourself after morning psalms not to go out from the place of your struggle without necessity before Terce. But take the Gospel and read while standing. Then set it with honour at its place and sit a little while by yourself in a corner and consider what has come upon you from the evening until morning. Then confess in your heart and glorify our Lord, who has preserved you from the Evil One and his hosts, and upheld you to accomplish His will. Then

---

[53] Joy (ḥadûtâ): there is mention of joy several times in this translation. It occurs often in the 'golden age' of Syriac Christian literature: Sahdona (early 7th c.), Isaac (late 7th c.), Dadisho (late 7th c.), Shem`on (late 7th c.), John of Dalyatha (mid 8th c.), Joseph Hazzaya (mid 8th c.). Whether it is ḥadûtâ or ḥadûtâ db-alâhâ: human joy or joy which is in God, seemingly of His very nature. In Isaac it may be linked to *theosis*, see Hansbury 'The Path of Joy in Isaac the Syrian'. Shem`on saw humans not only as an image of God but also as the 'bond of creation', with an approach to *theosis* inclusive of a mediatory position (link: *essârâ*) between God and the universe, influenced by Theodore of Mopsuestia. See Bettiolo, *Simone di Taibuteh. Violenza e grazia: la coltura del cuore*, 47. See also Mar Gregorios, *The Human Presence: ecological spirituality and the age of the spirit*, 93. McLeod comments on Christ's salvific role as the bond of the universe in Theodore of Mopsuestia, see his *The roles of Christ's Humanity in Salvation: Insights from Theodore of Mopsuestia*, 102–23. Shem`on connects both image of God and link to the universe in the context of mirror (*maḥzitâ*), see Mingana, *Shem`on the Graceful, Medico-Mystical Work*, 171b, 195b for this and for the 'bond of creation'. See also Khayyat, 'Le Visage du Christ resplendissant dans le miroir du coeur'.

[54] On the concept of grace (ṭaybûtâ) as it leads to the New Life (ḥayyê ḥadtê) see Kessel, 'La position de Simon de Taibuteh dans l'éventail de la tradition mystique syriaque', 131–3. In another work of Mar Shem`on, see Kessel, 'The Activity of Grace in the *Book of Grace*. Some Preliminary Observations', 57–68.

draw near to the Cross[55] and offer obeisance while kneeling. Pray and beseech God with sighs, that He send you help and strengthen you so that you might honourably celebrate all your Hours with care and diligence, according to the will of the Spirit. Again bow, and kneeling offer obeisance to the Cross. Take the book of the solitary Fathers, sit before the Cross and read a little. Then stand and pray, offering obeisance until Terce: read a little and pray a little, according to your strength.

12 Before Terce strikes anticipate it a little; stand for that Hour and celebrate it without distraction while you are there, with genuflections and prayers. Between each of your Hours read a little and pray a little in this way, until None. After None go into the refectory and prepare your food, whatever is found. A little before [eating] proceed to the evening Office, according to the usage of the monastery. Then, after the Office, enter the refectory and prepare the table with water and all which is useful for your needs. Even if only stale bread and salt are found, may your table be respectable in your eyes, like the table of Christ. Sanctify your table with prayers, with praises and with spiritual hymns, as is usual at the community table.

13 Go out to the courtyard and walk a little back and forth, with a peaceful step. Then return to the place of your struggle. Begin Compline and celebrate it without distraction, as the Fathers have written. Then when you lie down, recite: 'Who dwells in the refuge of the Most High in Glory';[56] and 'I lift up my eyes to the mountain to God my custodian',[57] and add: 'Day and night, glory to

---

[55] See Isaac II XI, 'On the contemplation of the mystery of the Cross …'. And see Alfeyev, *The Spiritual World of Isaac the Syrian*, 163–74. Alfeyev notes how at the time of Isaac in the absence of a 'developed tradition of icon-painting' the cross became a symbol of human salvation and of God's invisible presence. He quotes Isaac II XI.5 that the Shekhina once dwelt in the Old Testament Ark and now dwells in the New Testament cross; and Isaac II XI.24–6: 'For the cross is Christ's garment just as the humanity of Christ is the garment of the Divinity.' Insights such as these indicate the depth of devotion to the cross in Shem`on as well. The cross came to be considered as one of the seven Sacraments (*râzê*) by the East Syrian tradition. See Badger, *The Nestorians and their Rituals*, Appendix B: 'Mar Abd Yeshua, "The Jewel"', parts 4 & 5. See also Kollamparambil, 'Cross and Crucifix in the Syrian Tradition'.

[56] Ps. 90:1.

You, O God';[58] then the Trisagion, genuflection and prayers. Also, seal your prayer with the prayer of the 'Our Father who art in heaven', and 'May Your Cross, our Saviour, be for us a bulwark'. And until you have fallen asleep may prayer, intercession and thanksgiving not be far *from your mouth and your heart.*[59]

14 Watch and take heed! Do not yield the bed of the upright to iniquity! Understand what I say! When grace wakens you at midnight, rise up for prayer, diligently rouse your senses and your limbs. Burn incense if you have some and begin the Office as is the custom with quick genuflections, so that you are not overcome by sleep. If after the Office you are weak and there is time, sit in a corner before the Cross[60] and refresh yourself a little with prayer and with sleep. Then proceed with the morning psalms and pray for me.

15 Depict[61] continually in your mind the fourteen forms of conduct which Abba Isaiah set at the beginning of his discourse on the way of the virtues, which happen to the solitary in the quiet of the cell. This is the list: 'There is the fall—for also the enemies are there—there are variations, there are changes, there is abundance,

---

[57] Ps. 120:1.

[58] See the whole prayer as attributed to Abraham of Kashkar in Chialà and Nin, *Abramo di Kashkar, Giovanni il Solitario. Nell'umiltà e nella mitezza. Regole monastiche, lettera a esichio*, 19–20. See also the comments of Chialà in *Abitare la solitudine*, 22–3.

[59] Cf. Deut. 30:14.

[60] On the Cross, see also one of John of Dalyatha's Discourses: 'Sometimes when I am kissing the cross there shines from it upon my face a star of glorious and wondrous brightness, and my heart rejoices; and when I stretch out my hand and put it before me in the air or on my body I see it established in the likeness of an ineffable light. At the marvellous sight gladness is stirred up in my heart such as I have no strength in me to endure before it …'. (Discourse 3 Vat.Sir.124, 286 a–b) trans. Colless, *The Mystical Discourses of John Saba*, 162–3 and Beulay, *L'enseignement spirituel de Jean de Dalyatha*, 156–8. See also the comments on the Cross by Dadisho in Mingana *Treatise on Solitude and Prayer: On Seven Weeks of Solitude*, 51b–54b.

[61] Depict (ṣir from ṣûr): on the close connection between image and word in Syriac tradition see Griffith, 'The Image of the Image Maker in the Poetry of St. Ephrem the Syrian'.

there are quantities, there is privation, there is *acedia*, there is joy, there is affliction of the heart, there is sadness, there is the heart's rest, there is growth, there is coercion.[62]

16 Elucidation of 'There is the fall'. Concerning the fall and the enemies: it occurs if in your cell, without your willing it or from the infirmity of your nature, or again from the violence of hostile demons, that you are overcome and you lapse because of one of the passions. Do not be despondent or fall into despair. But rise up, act mightily in the Lord! Turn and show yourself strong in your struggle against the evil ones.

17 'There are changes', they occur to a solitary within the still-ness[63] of the cell, as also Abba Macarius wrote,[64] similar to the changes which happen in the air. At times there are clouds, at times sadness, which thickens within the heart and darkens the soul like a cloud which thickens in the air. And again it changes and there is serenity and joy of heart, as with the light of the sun.

O solitary, who dwells in stillness, see and understand what the Fathers wrote from their personal experience. Do not be foolish; when grace examines you by means of struggles, afflictions and temptations, do not be distressed beyond measure and fall into the hands of the enemies who seek your soul. Then at the time of rest, joy and consolation which comes to you from grace, do not be puffed up or haughty, lest you lose yourself.

---

[62] The Syriac text of Abba Isaiah is found in Draguet, *Les cinq recensions de l'Ascéticon syriaque d'Abba Isaïe, II. Logoi XIV–XXVI*, 362. References to Abba Isaiah occur throughout Letter 18 of John of Dalyatha, see Beulay, *La collection des lettres de Jean de Dalyatha.*

[63] Stillness (*šelyâ*).

[64] Macarius is quoted in the context of Isaac I XXII, on variations and changes. See also 'The First Syriac Epistle of Saint Macarius' in Miller, *The Ascetical Homilies of Saint Isaac the Syrian*, 562. See Beulay, *La lumière sans forme. Introduction a l'étude de la mystique chrétienne syro-orientale*, 202–6 on Macarian influence in Shem`on.

[65] Variations (*šuḥlâpê*): changes, afflictions, adversities, frequent sufferings,

18

'There are variations'.[65] When you change one conduct for another, and [one] labour for another, to add to your way of life and to your learning, do not be troubled nor grieved like foolish persons. Do not persist in former habits which have become easy for you but let go of what is easy and put in place other habits. Then ascend in the traditional order, as commanded by the Fathers. In fact, according to the word of Abba Isaiah and the Fathers, until the perfection of one's way of life, even though customs, labours and works are good, you may increase or diminish them as is usual in such a school, mother and nourisher of all.

19

'There is abundance, there is scarcity or [various] measures.' And if again abundance or measured quantities, or scarcity of what is necessary for use is provided for you, do not boast or become proud because of abundance, and in necessity let not your spirit be grieved or distressed like those who are untrained. But at a time of sadness, await joy. And at the time of joy and abundance, expect tribulations, because thereby this way of holiness is acquired. And whoever departs from this will be [prey] for wolves, said one of the saints.[66]

You then our beloved, in the stillness of your cell, be like a wise pilot who steers his ship in the midst of a strong and windy sea, and shows his skill against the accidents which occur in the sea air when against blowing winds he sometimes lowers the sails, then sometimes raising them again, and in every circumstance attempts to guide his boat to a quiet harbour, preserving it from the tossing of the waves. He is not puffed up with pride when a calm wind blows for him, and he does not despair of his life nor feel forsaken and flee

---

darkness of soul, depression, feelings of cold, tumult, gloom, doubt and despair of life. Shem῾on considers the awareness of these changes to be an essential part of solitary life. According to Isaac the Syrian, varied states occur for greater humility, being workings of God by his hidden Will (*remzâ kasyâ*), see Isaac II ix.6–12; xxiii.2; xxxv.3. John of Dalyatha speaks of them, including a need for a guide in the midst of *šuḥlâpê*, see his *Homélies*, vi.7; viii.9 in Khayyat, *Jean de Dalyatha, les homélies I–XV*. And see his Discourse 6, 'On the visitations bestowed on solitaries' in Colless, *The Mystical Discourses of John Saba*, 155–7.

[66] See Macarius as quoted in note 64 above.

when the waves and storms afflict him. He knows, indeed, that God guides everything in the sea and in the cell.

20 'There is *acedia*, there is joy.' Rightly did [Abba Isaiah] add joy to *acedia*. Indeed, all of the Fathers wrote in this way, that after severe *acedia* if the solitary remains in his cell, and babbles to our Lord with sighs, without ceasing from his struggle in the stillness of the cell, our Lord will cause great joy[67] to dwell in him with rest for the heart. But if he flees from the silent struggle, suffering of the heart and remorse with sadness will seize him.

21 'There is growth.' The solitary, however, is not fully formed in the Spirit, nor has he reached the full measure of perfection,[68] if by gradual growth he has not endured within stillness the violence of the demons, the fall and rising in the passions and the various temptations which affect him. Nor is he formed if he has not fallen and risen within stillness; and has not received in himself the experience of the fourteen forms of conduct written about by Abba Isaiah; and has not been brought up in spiritual growth in the presence of spiritual Fathers; and has not been raised up little by little from one way to another, from one labour to another and from knowledge to greater knowledge etc., by means of these ways.

22 'There is coercion.' [Abba Isaiah] calls coercion all the weapons with which the adversary besieges the solitaries who love stillness,[69] whether the battle of the demons or temptations

---

[67] Joy (*ḥadûtâ*): this mention of joy includes an intimation of the joy which is in God (*ḥadûtâ db-alâhâ*).

[68] Cf. Eph. 4:13.

[69] According to Alfeyev, stillness (*šelyâ*) and spiritual prayer (*ṣlôṯâ rûḥânâïtâ*) are synonyms in Isaac. Stillness is not acquired by human effort but is a gift of God. Further, one does not lose identity as it is a state of extreme activity, entirely under the power of God even when there is absence of movements of the mind yet there is never loss of personal existence rather an 'intense personal communion between a human person and a personal God'. See Alfeyev, *The Spiritual World of Isaac the Syrian*, 217–23. Wonder (*temhâ*) is involved, see Louf, '*Temha*-stupore e *tahra*-meraviglia negle scritti di Isacco il Siro'. See also Hansbury, '"Insight without Sight": Wonder as an Aspect of Revelation in the Discourses of Isaac the Syrian'. Brock

from nature or from a fellow creature or from any other side; or
whether it be the annoyance from the passions or the desires. And
every battle in which the solitary conquers or is overcome, necessi-
tating a struggle, is called coercion.

23 You then, our beloved in our Lord, if a slight *acedia* oppresses
you in the cell and casts you down and negligence holds
sway and thoughts come apart by chance; and if fear is taken away
from your heart and modesty be wiped from your face and the will
chafes in the face of necessities, take notice so that negligence not
suggest to you other than to go out from the cell, while *acedia* feigns
necessities and impels you to go out and the compulsion of habits
leads you out for worthless business.

So when from a little idleness *acedia* has begun, it brings forth in
us a dense forest of passions if from the beginning we do not cut off
the causes through the endurance of contentiousness, and with
earnest and tenacious prayers, calming within us the passions of the
soul which rise up against the virtues we have cultivated; with doubt,
pride and ostentation, awakening in us base, worldly passions: laxity,
licentiousness, chattering and familiarity.[70]

---

notes the close relationship of stillness and wonder, see Isaac II XII.1. See
also *Discorsi spirituali* IV.XCV in Bettiolo, *Isacco di Ninive. Discorsi spirituali:
capitoli sulla conoscenza, preghiere,* and mention of the Greek use (through
Theodore of Mopsuestia) of *temhâ,* whereas the Peshitta has *šelyâ.* In the
Discorsi spirituali there are over thirty-five examples of *šelyâ.* See de
Halleux, *Martyrius [Sahdona] Œuvres spirituelles, IV. Lettres à des amis solitaire, maximes sapientiales,* esp. Letter 5. See also Dadisho's *Discourse on
Solitude (šelyâ)* (Mingana, *Treatise on solitude and prayer: on seven weeks of
solitude.* Alfeyev notes the close semantic link between wonder and ine-
briation (*rawwîyûtâ*) which Isaac uses to describe 'an especially strong experience of the love of God,' *The Spiritual World of Isaac the Syrian,* 248–56.
See Isaac II X.35 for the references in Isaac and also in John the Solitary,
Sahdona and Dadisho', including Shem`on. See Mingana, *Shem`on the
Graceful, Medico-Mystical Work,* 189b; 190a, b. Finally, for Shem`on wonder
(*temhâ*) is linked to perfection (*šumlâyâ*); not personal effort alone, nor the
loss of it, but the power of God implicit in *temhâ* brings one to the perfection of love.

[70] Familiarity (Gr. *parresía*), excessive speech: see comments of Bettiolo,
Simone di Taibuteh. Violenza e grazia: la coltura del cuore, 148–9.

When force of habit by means of laxity, chattering and familiarity removes fear and modesty from the heart, then the soul has concealed its face and become a harlot without shame before onlookers, and does not fear God.[71]

Force of habit makes the sober one lustful, the silent one talkative and the thoughtful one not able to reflect. And when the limit of observance has been broken and endurance of torment has been uprooted; and [when] one who is honourable has become immodest and the will has yielded and confusion reigns, and the rules fixed for the cell are relaxed by circumstances, then the solitary is not different from a reed swayed by the wind of the various passions, casting him without pause all over from one side to another. Therefore, from the beginning one ought to contend and take pains forcefully against the passions of desire and *acedia*, lest our labour be in vain.

24 Also this I make known to your divine charity: before being afflicted and brought low, and falling and rising up in the labours of the body and soul, and knowing ourselves, that we are children of the earth, as it is written, 'You are dust and to dust you will return',[72] it is not right to consider the heights and imagine the exalted things of the saints, *children of the light*.[73]

Because, as our Fathers knew by experience and transmitted to us, the fear of God which is acquired by means of labours, temptations and humiliations, precedes the love for God which is strengthened by purity and limpidity of the soul. The cross of ignominy, spitting, *bitter herbs*[74] and the spear, precede the cross of life. The labours of the ascetic life precede the joy of the ascetic life. The *acedia*, losing heart and negligence of the cell, precede the tranquillity[75] of the cell. The battles,

---

[71] Cf. Prov. 7:6ff.

[72] Gen. 3:19.

[73] Eph. 5:8; 1 Thess. 5:5.

[74] Ex. 12:8; Num. 9:11; Matt. 27:34.

[75] Tranquillity, see 'place of tranquillity' (*'aṯrâ d-šaïnâ*) in John of Dalyatha, where he says it is the place of 'light without form' (*nuhrâ dlâ dmû*), Beulay,

afflictions and various temptations by which the solitary is tested, precede the fruits of the cell. The bondage of the passions and the work of the commandments that are done forcefully, precede the ways of liberty. While the moderation of the senses and guard of the heart[76] precede the ways of the mind.

25 For love which precedes fear is not different from a harlot who incites the soul, enslaving it by the desire of lofty ways and inflaming it with the fervour of the impulses and of approval from others, with illusions which the mind imagines is the truth. And before ascending the cross of ignominy, in the bitterness of constraining labours, one seeks to ascend the cross of life.

This is what the Fathers wrote: 'The anger of God comes on the one who, before ascending the cross of ignominy, seeks to ascend the cross of life.'[77] For it is written: 'What is of the Lord comes on its own if the place of the heart is not stained but pure.'[78]

26 Since Satan is jealous of what is pleasing and is convinced that the solitary is not able to know himself nor to *adore the Father in spirit and truth*[79] outside of stillness, as it is written; thus when he sees that the solitary truly dwells in the way of stillness of his own accord, he strikes him in the liver with an arrow. And as

---

La collection des lettres de Jean de Dalyatha, Letter 51.7. This Evagrian concept is noted in John's Discourse 6.15 where it is identified with the Holy Trinity, see Khayyat, *Jean de Dalyatha, les homélies I–XV*, 165. And see Beulay, *L'enseignement spirituel de Jean de Dalyatha*, 393–5. Perhaps Shem`on sees the cell as a place of the 'light without form'. See also Hansbury, *John the Solitary on the Soul*, 15 . In Mor A. Y. Samuel, ed., *M'ade'dono: The Book of the Church Festivals*, in the brief service of pardon at the beginning of Great Lent, there are twenty mentions of tranquility (*šaïnâ*), of the very nature of God or of Christ and one mention of the human heart as the habitation of tranquility.

[76] Guard of the heart (*nṭûrta d-lebbâ*), see Isaac II xxix.7; occurs not with human effort but only by converse with God (*'enyânâ d-'am alâhâ*).

[77] Abba Isaiah, Draguet, *Les cinq recensions de l'Ascéticon syriaque d'Abba Isaïe, II. Édition des logoi XIV-XXVI*, 405; *Les cinq recensions de l'Ascéticon syriaque d'Abba Isaïe, II. Version des logoi XIV-XXVI avec des parallèles Grecs*, 451.

[78] Isaac I ii (Bedjan, *Mar Isaacus, de perfectione religiosa*, 16–17), refers both to 'ascending the cross' and 'place of the heart'.

[79] John 4:24.

much as possible even beyond his [Satan's] strength, at all times, first by means of his forces—the solitary's indolent brethren—and in the end in person, he discloses himself to draw the solitary from the way of stillness and to lead him by a lofty way outside of stillness, a way which pleases many. Then, when the solitary is persuaded of this, slackening the limit of his vigilance and dwelling in the ways outside of stillness, Satan returns to him, serving his needs and supplying his necessities abundantly. Also, he brings to him many who praise him and who come to honour him. These things, and greater than these, the Evil One does against the solitary who loves the way of stillness.

27 You then brother, quick to discern, who have learned all of this from your Fathers who have experienced in themselves the deception of the devils and have perceived the mysteries of stillness; when your reflection deceives you to exchange the way of stillness for higher ways beyond stillness, before the fifteen years necessary for you to taste the grace of the mysteries hidden in stillness, do not obey your conscience but remember that every way whether of stillness or beyond stillness requires what is due.

And when you feel compelled by your reflection to substitute the ways of stillness and of observance with the ways of laxity and satisfaction of so many, and to substitute the hidden converse[80] in your inner being[81] with the familiarity of a life outside of stillness, do not

---

[80] Converse (*'enyânâ*), according to Evagrius: 'Prayer is the "converse" of the mind with God' (Bamberger, *Evagrius Ponticus. The Prakticos & Chapters on Prayer*, 56). Even within the Trinity it occurs, see Philoxenus: 'The converse of the Holy Spirit [which dwells within us] with God is the aim of all ascetic labours …' (Brock, *The Syriac Fathers on Prayer and the Spiritual Life*, 130). For Isaac: 'Just as nothing resembles God, so there is no ministry or work which resembles converse with God (*'enyânâ d-'am alâhâ*) in stillness' (Isaac II XXX.1). Shem`on takes it further to say that it makes one a man 'like unto' an angel (Bettiolo, *Simone di Taibuteh. Violenza e grazia: la coltura del cuore*, 36–7). John of Dalyatha speaks of the contacts and converse (*'enyânâ*) between angels and the soul (*Letters* 4.5, 19.6, 31.4). And see Hansbury, *The Letters of John of Dalyatha*, introd. xvii–xix. See also Beulay, *L'enseignement spirituel de Jean de Dalyatha*, 360–2. Isaac I V (Bedjan, *Mar Isaacus, de perfectione religiosa*, 65–7) describes delightful contacts between angels and humanity.

[81] Rom. 7:22; Eph. 3:16.

obey your conscience. Because as soon as we turn away from the inner ways and dwell in the ways outside, day by day, with the alteration of ways also habits and customs are changed as well as what is proper to stillness and the guard of the heart. We will acquire also the habits of relaxation and so be with all in familiarity and hypocritical love. And our familiarity with God[82] in hidden prayer will be changed in our familiarity with humans: little by little, in one way instead of another, one type of converse instead of another, one kind of familiarity instead of another, etc. It is inevitable that with the change of ways acquired even inner spiritual knowledge is transformed into knowledge of exterior realities. And with those there is also change, of contemplation with contemplation, intelligence with intelligence, meditation with meditation, memory with memory, thought with thought; advantage of the soul with advantage of the body, future hope with hope for the present, simplicity with cunning, divine love with human love, spiritual joy with worldly joy, honour which is from God with honour which is from humans, love for divine realities with love for human realities. Also, diligence and care for mystical realities is changed into diligence for visible realities.[83]

28 On this account, all love, whether for good or for evil, stirs up care in the soul for itself and separates [the soul] from desire of what opposes it. Now, for the heart which believes, justice done in the midst of many cannot be compared to being occupied with hidden

---

[82] On familiarity (*parresía*) with God see the explanation of Bettiolo, *Simone di Taibuteh. Violenza e grazia: la coltura del cuore*, 148–9. And see Isaac I xxxv (Bedjan, *Mar Isaacus, de perfectione religiosa*, 265): 'familiarity with Him and knowledge of His mysteries'.

[83] This paragraph is an indirect way of understanding how the Syriac tradition understood ascetical life in a transformative way not simply as denial, for example, of human love but exchanging it for an even greater reality. Here is indicated the reverse, denying divine reality for human reality. The Syriac Fathers saw the importance of transformation rather than extirpation. See Hansbury, *The Letters of John of Dalyatha*, Letter 47 and Hansbury, trans., *John the Solitary on the Soul*, Introd. 'Passions'. See also Beulay, *La lumière sans forme*, 202–6.

prayer[84] which is done with God within stillness. The mind which is perverted from stability with Christ does not perceive the mysteries of the Spirit which are raised up for the saints within stillness.

As nothing is comparable to God, nor is there justice comparable to being occupied in prayer with God, which sanctifies the solitary and makes him a man [like unto] an angel.[85]

29 You then, our brother, train your soul to practice the virtues faithfully, with force. The kneeling prayers, especially, are always in need of force. And for this, the beginning of all ways, as the Fathers testify, is the way of force which controls the solitary at every moment and continually gives him the *bitter herbs*[86] of force to drink and restrains him from the desire of his will.

By the way of force, wickedness is uprooted from the soul, the commandments are observed and the passions overcome. By the *bitter herbs* of force the heart is broken and the soul brought low to receive the reins of fear and modesty. By the painful ways of force, manners, habits, qualities and disorderly behaviour cease, changed from what is unnatural to what is natural.

With great force the solitary must cut off converse with others and become accustomed to constant tranquillity in his cell. He must force himself to keep the commandments of the Fathers and the rules of the cell which are, briefly, the seven appointed Hours, the prayers as specified, diverse readings, meditation on divine things, custody of the heart, nightly vigils, also to be vigilant and prudent in the cell of one's heart. One ought not to receive strange thoughts and worthless memories but to persevere in the evening fast and not to neglect manual work which binds us to the cell and removes from us laziness and *acedia*, etc.

---

[84] Hidden prayer (*ṣlôtâ kasyûṭâ*).

[85] Literally, 'makes him an angel-man' (*mal'ak barnâšâ*). As noted by Bettiolo in *Simone di Taibuteh. Violenza e grazia: la coltura del cuore*, 36, according to tradition the 'angelic way' is that of the solitary giving glory to God, proclaiming 'holy, holy, holy', like the angels, Isaiah 6:3. See also Beulay, *L'enseignement spirituel*, 363–8. And see Isaac II VIII.6 where the mode of life of the angels is compared to life after the resurrection. Cf. above note 80.

[86] Ex. 12:8; Num. 9:11.

With great force the solitary cuts off his hope from the world and its desires and binds his memory to the New World[87] and its glories.

Thus the pleasing habits acquired with force, when they have been acquired, in the end will also fight against the passions of sin.

30 Habit strengthens everything for good or for evil. When good habits take hold in the heart, they make a sinner a just one. And when evil habits take possession of the soul, they make the just one a sinner. Habits are the chains that bind the soul and which are easily acquired but dissolved with difficulty. Habits require what they are accustomed to and what makes them strong. When a habit takes hold in a person, just as nature compulsively requires nourishment, drink and sleep, so also habit compulsively requires what is its own, whether for good or for evil.

31 You then, our beloved, if you wish to be freed from the annoyance of the passions and that the fruits of the cell might be seen in you, cut yourself off charitably from everything and close your senses from noise in the constant tranquillity of your cell. Enter into your cell and persevere inside yourself, within your *inner being*;[88] bear with a grateful heart what occurs there providentially. Do not give space to shifting memories or changing thoughts but calm yourself by trusting in God and with the reading of Scripture. Because as manual work binds the body to the cell, likewise also converse in one's *inmost self*[89] in prayer with God, binds the impulses of the soul to the cell of the heart, lest they wander among vain things.

---

[87] New World (*'âlmâ ḥadtâ*): the phrase which derives from Peshitta Matt. 19:28 is especially common in John the Solitary. See also Evagrius (*'âlmâ da-'tîd*) *Kephalaia Gnostica* VI.39, 81 [S. 1] (Guillaumont, *Évagre le Pontique. Les six centuries des 'Kephalaia Gnostica'*). And see Isaac II v.5 for references in Isaac. *'âlmâ ḥadtâ* occurs in Hansbury, *The Letters of John of Dalyatha* and also in his Discourse 12 'On the mystery of the New World', Vat.sir.124, 329a–b.

[88] Inner being (*barnâšâ gawwâyâ*): Isaac II VIII.2, 'The ascetic conduct of the inner person is a symbol of existence after the resurrection ...', and see Bettiolo, *Isacco di Ninive. Discorsi spirituali*, IV.60.

[89] Ephesians 3:16.

32 Be it remembered always that saying which Abba Poemen spoke to the brothers: 'All virtues have entered the house of our heart, except this: that we accuse ourselves. This guards all the virtues, acquired with ascetic labours.'[90] This is what the blessed Apostle wrote; 'If only we judge ourselves, we will not be judged.'[91]

The demons are not able to remind the solitary, who in his cell condemns himself, of the infirmities of his brothers. One of the saints trustworthy in the Spirit said: 'The voluntary prison which is the furnace of the cell of the saints, the vexations of asceticism; enticements which torture the heart; afflictions which consume the soul; passions which torment the intelligence; the battles and temptations which trouble the mind; derision and scorn; the insults which ascetics willingly endure from foolish persons; harm done by demons; the pains and infirmities which saints endure in the furnace of the cell, such as this is imputed to our Lord as He suffers with them in all their afflictions.'

33 Our Lord is truthful:[92] the New Creation[93] is the inner world of Christians; and those who do the commandments and have fairly conquered the passions in part, and whose heart has been purified with God's help, at the time of prayer new heavens[94] are engraved in their hearts.

Their death from the world, indeed, has prepared for them an inner world; and the torments of the senses and the impulses they have endured for this truth have granted them hidden consolation. Ignominy, derision and buffeting which they have endured from the dissolute, have crowned their minds with glory.[95] And the self-contempt and intellectual simplicity that willingly they showed for

---

[90] Poemen 134 in Budge, *The Paradise of the Holy Fathers*, II, 296: and II, 217. Cf. Ward, *The Sayings of the Desert Fathers*, 186.

[91] 1 Cor. 11:31.

[92] Cf. Titus 1:2.

[93] 2 Cor. 5:17; Gal. 6:15.

[94] Rev. 21:1.

[95] Literally, 'have placed on the head of the mind a crown of glory', Cf. 2 Tim. 4:7–8.

this truth, prepared within them spiritual knowledge[96] and the gentleness of the angels of light.[97]

However, the inner world of the Spirit is not elevated, nor does it illumine the air of a heart's firmament which the cloud of passions veils, as long as the soul is bound voluntarily by love for one of the passions. Christ the *sun of justice*,[98] who dwells in the heart, does not shine forth except by complete trust in Him.

34 But because God is merciful,[99] He seeks the occasion to justify us and to offer us His gifts when one constrains himself and ardently desires divine joy for himself and cuts off hope in the world and all which concerns it, and lives in the absence of all human converse, standing continually before His majesty in converse with Him: in mystery, in prayer, intercession, supplication, prostrations, tears, a broken heart; giving thanks, in remembrance of the way of life of the holy *children of light*,[100] with the mind's earnest desire. Then truly, the inner door of the Holy of Holies will be opened for the consolation of one's own simplicity, and the cloud of passions will be mercifully dispelled from before the firmament of the mind. The air of one's heart will glisten, the eyes of the mind will be opened to behold mystically, in the light of faith, the mysteries of the Spirit which are celebrated within us.[101] Then the solitary, amazed, will confess and glorify God.

---

[96] Chialà suggests here instead of being seen as experts in knowledge, they receive spiritual knowledge, *Abitare la solitudine*, 35.

[97] 2 Cor. 11:14.

[98] Mal. 3:20; Luke 1:78.

[99] Cf. Luke 6:36.

[100] Eph. 5:8; 1 Thess. 5:5.

[101] On the mysteries that the Spirit celebrates 'within us', in Aphrahat some beautiful things are said about interior prayer and the soul as 'hidden church', *Demonstrations* IV,11–13 as found in Brock, *The Syriac Fathers on Prayer and the Spiritual Life*, 5–25. This intensifies in the *Book of Steps*, XII, 2–3 with the 'altar of the heart', *The Syriac Fathers*, 45–59. Sahdona hints at the liturgy of the heart and the soul as 'hidden church', *Book of Perfection* III.57 found in *The Syriac Fathers*, 226. And in Isaac I XXII (translated in *The Syriac Fathers*, 252–63) there is prayer of the heart as an internalized celebration of the Eucharist, on the altar of the heart.

35 You then, our beloved, if you have received mercy and by grace you have begun to taste the mysteries of the Spirit, and the sweetness of the cell has begun to draw you to itself from everything else, then be attentive to the deceit of the envious Evil One.[102]

Because when the Evil One sees a solitary with a strong soul who has cut himself off from all obstacles and has cast behind his body, honour or insult, praise or blame; and in the angelic way of stillness has lifted the sail of his heart towards the life-giving Cross; and has armed himself as an athlete with faith, hope and love;[103] and has joined together fasting, asceticism, nightly vigils, various readings, the Office, prayers, intercessions, tears,[104] and thanksgiving; so that with the earnest desire of his heart he always hopes and awaits the operation of grace[105] so that the eyes of his mind be opened by the Spirit, so that he might become strong in hope and made perfect in love and be unified by the mystery hidden within and by means of contemplation perceive mystically in the light of faith the revelations of knowledge; then the Evil One is irritated and attempts even beyond his power to cut off these occasions of grace by means of satanic obstacles.

But if, though having increased his plots and having schemed and entreated God, by divine providence he is not permitted to impede our

---

[102] Cf. Wisd. 2:24.

[103] 1 Cor. 13:13.

[104] On tears at an advanced stage, see Isaac I IV, VI, XIV (Bedjan 49, 93, 125–6). Tears and weeping occur frequently in Isaac II, see the indexes (Brock, *Isaac of Nineveh (Isaac the Syrian). 'The Second Part', Chapters IV-XLI*, vol. II). John the Solitary dedicates three pages to a discussion of tears, Hansbury, *John the Solitary on the Soul*, 16–18. Beulay looks at tears of repentance and tears of joy and wonder, comparing John of Dalyatha and John the Solitary and how tears come during the stage of limpidity, see Beulay, *L'enseignement spirituel de Jean de Dalyatha*, 201–5.

[105] Operation of grace (*ma'bdânûtâ d-ṭaybûtâ*): on the complexity of the concept of grace in Shem'on, see Kessel's 'La position de Simon de Taibuteh dans l'éventail de la tradition mystique syriaque', 131–9. Kessel discusses the mystery of grace (*râzâ d-ṭaybûtâ*) and how it relates to created knowledge and even to the knowledge of Scripture (138). See also Kessel, 'The Activity of Grace in the *Book of Grace*. Some Preliminary Observations'.

path towards truth, then he changes to be like one who helps our way of life and supplies what is necessary to fulfil labours while inflaming the will in the vehemence of bodily labours and stirring the mind with profound reading, subtle understanding and exalted contemplation for the love of new things, etc. This is his goal: either that the harp[106] be fettered with which we practice the virtues and our course be hindered, or that [our] temperament be ravaged, or that the brain be injured and troubled and be in need of many things which are against our goal. Or because of the beauty of our virtues, we scorn the weak and exalting ourselves we fall by Satan's verdict and are mocked by the demons. As it is written in the book of Paradise concerning Valens the Palestinian, Ahrôn the Alexandrian, Ptolemy the Egyptian, Stephen the Ascetic, Eucarpus the Silent, James the Wanderer and Wonder-Worker, and the others who became proud, were abandoned by divine providence and having fallen were brought low by lapses.[107] Their falling was for the rising of many in every generation.[108]

36 What will we do, then, we wretched ones, in that our Lord and the apostles and the Fathers, by means of these afflictions, inner and outer, trod in that *narrow way which leads to the new life*?[109] Within [there is] the violent battle with the passions and lusts which excite the soul and torment the heart. From outside [there is] the battle of the demons who hiss and lead into error and make us lapse from the truth, seeming to be virtuous.

37 Listen, my beloved: our Lord Himself, in His becoming man, prepared for us by means of His life-giving commandments a way full of grace, mercy and forgiveness of offenses. Instead of:

---

[106] 'The Harp' of the body, cf. Evagrius, *Kephalia Gnostica* 6.72 (Guillaumont, *Évagre le Pontique. Les six centuries des 'Kephalaia Gnostica'*), see Bettiolo, *Simone di Taibuteh. Violenza e grazia: la coltura del cuore*, 161.

[107] Cf. Draguet, *Les formes Syriaques de la matière de l'histoire lausiaque*, 307–8.

[108] Chialà suggests the sense here is that their falling as narrated in *The Paradise of the Holy Fathers* served to help others avoid the same sin; Chialà, *Abitare la solitudine*, 38.

[109] Matt. 7:14.

An eye for an eye and a blow for a blow,[110] He established new commandments opposed to these, such as not to requite evil for evil[111] but to
overcome the evil of your brother with your own goodness.

But if truly you long for the operation of grace so that the eyes of
your mind[112] be opened by the Spirit, and you be perfected in hope
and fulfilled in love, and that you might perceive the mystery of the
revelations[113] of spiritual knowledge:[114] overcome the wickedness of
others by your own goodness, their bitterness with your sweetness,
their wicked instinct with the limpidity of your knowledge according
to the new commandments, and the wickedness of their intelligence
with your mercy in the image of God. Be similar to God who shelters
and has mercy on the good and the wicked![115]

38 When, from the beginning of your dwelling in the cell, you
begin to change the growth of the natural habits in which you
were raised into new ways: labour into labour, knowledge into knowledge, hope into hope, love of the things of this life into love of the

---

[110] Ex. 21:24–5; Matt. 5:38–42.

[111] Rom. 12:17, 21; 1 Thess. 5:15.

[112] Eph. 1:18.

[113] Revelations (*gelyânê*): as noted by Alfeyev, in Isaac 'revelation refers to
the inner contiguity of a person with an earthly reality; it does not neces-
sarily presuppose seeing a certain visible image'. See *The Spiritual World of
Isaac the Syrian*, 229–36.

[114] Spiritual knowledge (*îdâtâ d-ruh*): see Isaac's gnoseology; his teaching
on the degrees of knowledge includes discussion of worldly knowledge;
commandments and asceticism; spiritual knowledge. See Alfeyev, *The
Spiritual World of Isaac the Syrian*, 256–68. 'There is knowledge that precedes
faith, and there is a knowledge born of faith. Knowledge that precedes faith
is natural knowledge; and that which is born of faith is spiritual knowledge'. 'Spiritual knowledge is, as we have said, that of which we received
the pledge in baptism and which we receive really by repentance
(*tyâbûtâ*)'. See Isaac I XLIV, LI, LII (Bedjan, 318–21, 360–77, 378–9), and see
Hansbury, 'The Concept of Faith in Isaac the Syrian in the Context of Early
Syriac Theology', being a discussion of faith as the highest form of knowledge and actually a quality of God, of his very nature that he shares with
his creatures. See also Vesa, *Knowledge and Experience in the Writings of St.
Isaac of Nineveh*.

[115] Cf. Matt. 5:44; Luke 6:35–6.

world to come, joy in visible realities into the joy of the Spirit, consolation into consolation, mercy into mercy; according to the new and spiritual commandments: *Love your enemies and bless who curse you,*[116] etc. Nature subject to passion, prone to evil, is not able to acquire and guard these realities while dwelling together with many others.

However, in the separation characteristic of stillness, in the prolonged converse in our inner being,[117] what was unnatural is easily changed into what is natural. Because we do not seek what is not of our nature, rather what we have lost with the transgression of the commandment by our father Adam and that we have recovered in Christ, our second father.

39 In fact, as soon as our father Adam transgressed the commandment his heart was defiled by the passions, and what was natural became unnatural. The inner door of the knowledge of spiritual mysteries closed and the inner spiritual being became blind, unable to see in a natural way his personal infirmities; instead, the inner being received the power to discern in an unnatural way the good and evil aspects of his nature. But while blinded by the passions from seeing naturally his own flaws, he became a wicked judge discerning the weaknesses of his neighbour.

From when, however, *the sun of justice has shone forth,*[118] our Lord the Christ has opened the inner door of the Holy of Holies of the heart and has prepared for us the way of the new life[119] by means of His life-giving commandments, the pillars of the Church.[120] And the philosophers of the Spirit, the solitary Fathers, have run there and have been constant in their inner being. They have found within

---

[116] Matt 5:44; Luke 6:28.

[117] Rom. 7:22; Eph. 3:16.

[118] Mal. 3:20; Luke 1:78.

[119] New life (*ḥayyê ḥadtê*): see note 51. John the Solitary interprets the whole history of salvation and the nature of the spiritual life according to the hope in the New World, influenced by Theodore of Mopsuestia. If after baptism, one remains in a state of spiritual growth, one is already in the new life of the New World.

[120] Gal. 2:9; 1 Tim. 3:5.

themselves the treasure of life and have enlightened the whole earth with their sound doctrine.

40 The continual converse of our hidden person[121] vivifies the dead soul and gives sight to the blind intelligence, purifies the unclean heart, recollects the wandering intellect, changes grief into joy, gives order to the senses, calms the impulses, renews the remembrance of thoughts, enlightens understanding, lifts up contemplation, makes discernment truthful,[122] strengthens the will, reconciles those to the right and pulls down those to the left, and makes entirely spiritual the natural heart by means of the divine mysteries which shine in the heart in a hidden way.

However, before the solitary pacifies the raging of his passions with voluntary labours and straightens according to nature what is unnatural in his person, if he imagines the lofty things of the saints he cultivates the passions of his desire and not the truth. Indeed, to know the truth is for all, even the tax-collectors and prostitutes,[123] because it is sown in our created nature; and to learn the truth or to teach the truth is an art of the soul, since the heart is the market place of the soul where good and evil things are practiced. But to accomplish in ourselves in deeds the truth we know and teach is impossible without good will, compulsion, labours, prayers, diligence and the action of grace.

41 You then, our beloved in our Lord, when you sit fittingly in your cell, consider the changes which occur in you by means of grace. And when understanding from the reading diverts you from manual work, yield to it and glorify God, because grace has begun to draw you to itself. And when you experience the sweetness of the labours of conversion: the Office, prayers, reading,[124] spiritual

---

[121] Cf. 1 Pet. 3:4. Hidden person (*barnâšâ kasyâ*).

[122] Literally: 'unites truth to discernment'.

[123] Cf. Matt. 21:31–2.

[124] Reading (*qeryânâ*): the most striking influence on Isaac the Syrian, at least in Isaac III, is Scripture. From reading (*qeryânâ*), limitless prayer (*ṣlôtâ*) is generated (IX.12) and the reading of Scripture is intended. Reading is for

meditation; be attentive to yourself, for grace has begun to effect within you its hidden mysteries. And when in the midst of prayer, the Office and reading, the love of Christ so burns in your heart that the gift of God hinders even the remembrance of thoughts, here avoid the deceit of the Evil One.

42 The heart which is broken by afflictions and suffers with compunction marvels greatly at these realities which attract from distraction. As long as the eye of your intelligence gazes at your heart and you consider with understanding your prayers, your Office and your petitions, the soul does not cease from sighs and you will be freed from the captivity of distraction.

Blessed is the solitary who chants and sings praise while standing there! And while you increase in love for others and overlook the infirmities of your neighbour from your heart, the sign of humility in you is great. But as long as you separate the tares from the grains of wheat,[125] this is a sign of pride. And as long as you are angry with the weak, you are a disciple of Moses. As long as your heart requires justice of others, you are deceived by the Evil One in the semblance of virtue. As long as you do good to the good and abhor sinners, you are not like Jesus.

And this is surprising, that while the path to the house of our Lord teaches limpidity, without a little deprivation, coercion and flight, it is not possible to keep the rules of the cell.

43 Also this I make known to your divine charity: as long as compunction for your transgressions has not refined your heart persist in virtues, because when compunction ceases to reprove and remind you, you quietly do hateful things.

---

prayer (IX.30). Reading is meditation (*hergâ*) and prayer. Prayer without reading is weak (IX.15). There is Evagrian influence in Isaac and even for Evagrius, Scripture was everything: 'it was not about finding a suitable garnish for his theological speculations or merely an aspect of monastic pedagogy. It was a mode of being, a keying himself into texts recited by heart day in and day out'. See Stewart, 'Imageless Prayer and the Theological Vision of Evagrius Ponticus', 199–201.

[125] Cf. Matt. 13:24–30.

The vine of the solitary is his heart. And the diligent solitary for the vine of his heart must show all the work and care that a vine-dresser must do and show for his vine: not only to cleanse the weeds of the passions [but to] hoe, fertilize and water, and especially to prune the vine-shoots of the heart, that are the virtues. [This is necessary] so that the vine-shoots of the heart not come up and bring forth too much fruit, beyond measure, and the root dry up quickly from the abundance of fruits and the ignorance of the vinedresser.[126]

Pruning of the heart of the solitary includes: afflictions, temptations, privation, insults, struggles, falls, getting lost, lapses, regret, disgust, *acedia,* injury, scorn, stoning with the tongue, diseases, infirmities, etc. These things from time to time providentially come to our aid, lest the heart be haughty with the success of the good deeds and fall by Satan's condemnation.

44 What I observe is that humans are not different from a double vessel[127] which inside is filled with a honeycomb and outside is full of bitter herbs. As long as [the solitary] is immersed and sunk in stillness close to his inner person, he consumes the divine sweetness which is hidden and at work in the heart. But when he is scattered in outer wandering, the weeds smother him and he eats the bitter herbs of the enticements of desires. And surprisingly, the bitter herbs of the outer wandering are more pleasing to the heart than the divine sweetness which is at work within us.

45 May glory, exaltation and worship be to God, and His mercy and compassion be poured forth in our assembly, now and always, forever and ever. Amen, amen.

---

[126] Cf. John 15:1–17.
[127] Cf. Matt. 23:25.

KEY WORDS ACCORDING TO PARAGRAPHS (INCLUDING NOTES)

BIBLICAL REFERENCES IN PARAGRAPHS

BIBLIOGRAPHY

PRIMARY SOURCES

MANUSCRIPTS

Biblioteca Apostolica Vaticana Vat.sir.509
     (https://digi.vatlib.it/view/MSS_Vat.sir.509)
Biblioteca Apostolica Vaticana Vat.sir.124
     (https://digi.vatlib.it/view/MSS_Vat.sir.124)

TRANSLATIONS AND EDITIONS

Abba Isaiah

R. Draguet, trans. and ed., *Les cinq recensions de l'Ascéticon syriaque d'Abba Isaïe, I. Les témoins et leurs parallèles non-syriaques. Édition des Logoi I-XIII*, Corpus Scriptorum Christianorum Orientalium, 289/Scriptores Syri, 120; *II. Édition des Logoi XIV-XXVI*, Corpus Scriptorum Christianorum Orientalium, 290/Scriptores Syri, 121 (Louvain: Peeters, 1968).

———, *Les cinq recensions de l'Ascéticon syriaque d'Abba Isaïe, I. Introduction au problème Isaïen. Version des Logoi I-XIII avec des parallèles Grecs et Latins*, Corpus Scriptorum Christianorum Orientalium, 293/Scriptores Syri, 122; *avec des parallèles Grecs, index*, Corpus Scriptorum Christianorum Orientalium, 294/Scriptores Syri, 123 (Louvain: Peeters, 1968).

Abraham of Kashkar

S. Chialà and M. Nin, trans. and ed., *Abramo di Kashkar, Giovanni il Solitario. Nell'umiltà e nella mitezza. Regole monastiche, lettera a esichio*, Testi dei Padri della Chiesa, 45 (Magnano, Monastero di Bose: Edizioni Qiqajon, 2000).

Aḥudemmeh

F. Nau, ed., *Les Histoires d'Ahoudemmeh et de Marouta, primats jacobites de Tagrit et de l'Orient (VIe-VIIe siècle), suivi du traité d'Aboudemmeh sur l'Homme*, Patrologia Orientalis, 11 (3.1) (Turnhout: Brepols, 1905), 101–15.

Dadisho' Qatraya

A. Mingana, trans. and ed., *Treatise on Solitude and Prayer: On Seven Weeks of Solitude*, Early Christian Mystics, Woodbrooke Studies, 7 (Cambridge: Heffer and Sons Ltd, 1934), 70–143.

R. Draguet, ed., *Commentaire du livre d'Abba Isaïe par Dadiso Qatraya (VIIe siè-cle)*, Corpus Scriptorum Christianorum Orientalium, 326–7/Scrip-tores Syri, 144–5 (Louvain: Peeters, 1972).

Desert Fathers

E. A. W. Budge, *The Paradise or Garden of the Holy Fathers: Being Histories of the Anchorites, Recluses, Monks, Coenobites, and Ascetic Fathers of the Deserts of Egypt Between A.D. 250 and A.D. 400*, 2 vols (London: Chatto & Windus, 1907; repr. Blanco TX: New Sarov Press, 1994).

B. Ward, trans., *The Sayings of the Desert Fathers: The Alphabetic Collection* (Kalamazoo: Cistercian Publications and Oxford: Mowbray, 1975).

St Ephrem

S. P. Brock, trans., *Ephrem the Syrian: Hymns on Paradise*, St Vladimir's Sem-inary Press Popular Patristics Series, 10 (Crestwood NY: St Vladimir's Seminary Press, 1997).

M. T. Hansbury, trans., *Hymns of St. Ephrem the Syrian*, Fairacres Publications, 149 (Oxford: SLG Press, 2006, repr. 2018).

E. G. Mathews and J. P. Amar, trans., *Saint Ephrem the Syrian: Selected Prose Works*, ed. by K. E. McVey, Fathers of the Church, 91 (Washington DC: Catholic University of America Press, 1994).

Evagrius Ponticus

J. E. Bamberger, trans., *Evagrius Ponticus. The Prakticos & Chapters on Prayer*, Cistercian Studies, 4 (Kalamazoo MI: Cistercian Publications, 1970, repr. 1989).

A. Guillaumont, ed., *Évagre le Pontique. Les six centuries des 'Kephalaia Gnostica'*, Patrologia Orientalis, 134 (28.1) (Turnhout: Brepols, 1958, repr. 1985).

Histoire Lausiaque

R. Draguet, trans. and ed., *Les formes Syriaques de la matière de l'histoire lau-siaque, II. Version des ch. 20–71, épilogue, appendice [72–73]*, Corpus Scriptorum Christianorum Orientalium, 398/Scriptores Syri, 174 (Louvain: Peeters, 1978).

Isaac the Syrian/Isaac of Nineveh

P. Bedjan, trans. and ed., *Mar Isaacus, de perfectione religiosa* (Paris/Leipzig: Otto Harrassowitz, 1909).

P. Bettiolo, trans. and ed., *Isacco di Ninive. Discorsi spirituali: capitoli sulla conoscenza, preghiere, contemplazione sull'argomento della gehenna, altri opuscoli*, Padri orientali (Magnano, Monastero di Bose: Edizioni Qiqajon, 1985; 2nd edn, 1990).

S. P. Brock, trans., *Isaac of Nineveh (Isaac the Syrian). 'The Second Part', Chapters IV-XLI*, Corpus Scriptorum Christianorum Orientalium, 554–5 / Scriptores Syri, 224–5 (Louvain: Peeters, 1995).

——, *The Wisdom of St. Isaac of Nineveh*, Texts from Christian Late Antiquity, 1 (Piscataway: Gorgias Press, 3rd edn 2006)

——, *The Wisdom of Saint Isaac the Syrian*, Fairacres Publications, 128 (Oxford: SLG Press, 1997, 7th edn 2018).

S. Chialà, trans. and ed., *Isacco di Ninive. Terza collezione*, Corpus Scriptorum Christianorum Orientalium, 637–8 / Scriptores Syri, 246–7 (Louvain: Peeters, 2011).

M. T. Hansbury, trans., *Isaac the Syrian's Spiritual Works (III, V)*, Texts from Christian Late Antiquity, 45 (Piscataway: Gorgias Press, 2016).

——, *St. Isaac of Nineveh. On Ascetical life* (New York: St Vladimir's Seminary Press, 1989), Part I, ch. 1–6.

A. Louf, trans., *Isaac le Syrien. Œuvres spirituelles II. Discours récemment découverts*, Spiritualité Orientale, 81 (Bégrolles-en-Mauges: Éditions de Bellefontaine, 2003).

——, *Isaac le Syrien. Œuvres spirituelles III. D'après un manuscrit récemment découvert*, Spiritualité Orientale, 88 (Bégrolles-en-Mauges: Éditions de Bellefontaine, 2009).

——, '*Temha*-stupore e *tahra*-meraviglia negle scritti di Isacco il Siro', in *La grande stagione della mistica siro-orientale (VI-VIII secolo). Atti del 5° Incontro sull'Oriente cristiano di tradizione siriaca, Milano, Biblioteca ambrosiana, 26 maggio 2006*, ed. by Emido Vergani and S. Chialà (Milan: Centro Ambrosiano, 2010), 93–119.

D. Miller, trans., *The Ascetical Homilies of Saint Isaac the Syrian*, (Boston: The Holy Transfiguration Monastery, 2011).

A. J. Wensinck, trans., *Mystic Treatises by Isaac of Nineveh*, Verhandelingen Der Koninklijke Akademie van Wetenschappen te Amsterdam. Afdeeling Letterkunde, Nieuwe Reeks, 23.1 (Amsterdam: De Akademie, 1923; repr. Wiesbaden, 1969), Part I.

Jacob of Serug

M. T. Hansbury, ed., *The Prayers of Jacob of Serugh*, Fairacres Publications, 177 (Oxford: SLG Press, 2015).

A. C. McCollum, trans. and ed., *Jacob of Sarug's Homilies on Jesus' Temptation*, Texts from Christian Late Antiquity, 38 (Piscataway: Gorgias Press, 2014).

T. Kollamparampil, trans., 'Homily on the Presentation' in *The Metrical Homilies of Mar Jacob of Sarug*, Texts from Christian Late Antiquity, 15, (Piscataway: Gorgias Press, 2008), Part 7.

——, *Jacob of Serugh, Select Festal Homilies* (Bangalore: Dharmaram Publications, 1997).

C. A. Scott and M. Reed, trans., *Jacob of Sarug's Homilies on the Solitaries*, Texts from Christian Late Antiquity, 41 (Piscataway: Gorgias Press, 2016).

John the Solitary/John of Apamea

M. T. Hansbury, trans., *John the Solitary on the Soul,* Texts from Christian Late Antiquity, 32 (Piscataway: Gorgias Press, 2013).

R. Lavenant, trans., *Jean d'Apamée. Dialogues et traités*, Sources Chrétiennes, 311 (Paris: Éditions du Cerf, 1984).

John of Dalyatha

B. E. Colless, trans., *The Mystical Discourses of John Saba* (University of Melbourne, unpublished dissertation, 1969) https://minerva-access.unimelb.edu.au/handle/11343/35391 (accessed 3 Feb 2020).

R. Beulay, trans., *La collection des lettres de Jean de Dalyatha*, Patrologia Orientalis, 180 (39.3) (Turnhout: Brepols, 1978).

M. T. Hansbury, trans., *The letters of John of Dalyatha*, Texts from Christian Late Antiquity, 2 (Piscataway: Gorgias Press, 2006).

N. Khayyat, ed. and trans., *Jean de Dalyatha, les homélies I–XV*, Sources Syriaques, 2 (Antélias, Liban: Centre d'Études et de Recherches Orientales, 2007).

Joseph Hazzaya

M. Albert, ed., *Joseph Ḥazzayâ. Lettre sur les trois étapes de la vie monastique*, trans. by P. Harb and F. Graffin, Patrologia Orientalis, 202 (45.2) (Turnhout: Brepols, 1992).

V. Lazzeri, trans., *Giuseppe Ḥazzayâ. Le tappe della vita spirituale* (Magnano, Monastero di Bose: Edizioni Qiqajon, 2011).

Nestorians and their Rituals

G. P. Badger, *The Nestorians and their Rituals, with the Narrative of a Mission to Mesopotamia and Coordistan in 1842-1844 and of a late visit to those Countries in 1850* (London: Joseph Masters, 1852).

Rabbinics

G. Friedlander, trans., *Pirke de Rabbi Eliezer: The Chapters of Rabbi Eliezer the Great*, The Judaic Studies Library, 6 (New York: Sepher-Hermon Press, 1981, 4th edn.).

Sahdona

A. de Halleux, trans., *Martyrius [Sahdona] Œuvres spirituelles, I. Livre de la perfection, 1e partie*, Corpus Scriptorum Christianorum Orientalium, 200–1/Scriptores Syri, 86–7 (Louvain: Peeters, 1960).

——, *Martyrius [Sahdona] Œuvres spirituelles, II. Livre de la perfection, 2e partie (ch. 1–7)*, Corpus Scriptorum Christianorum Orientalium, 214–5/Scriptores Syri, 90–1, (Louvain: Peeters, 1961).

——, *Martyrius [Sahdona] Œuvres spirituelles, III. Livre de la perfection, 2e partie (ch. 8–14)*, Corpus Scriptorum Christianorum Orientalium, 252–3/Scriptores Syri, 110–11 (Louvain: Peeters, 1965).

——, *Martyrius [Sahdona] Œuvres spirituelles, IV. Lettres à des amis solitaire, maximes sapientiales*, Corpus Scriptorum Christianorum Orientalium, 254–5/Scriptores Syri, 112–13 (Louvain: Peeters, 1965).

Shem`on the Graceful

P. Bettiolo, trans., *Simone di Taibuteh. Violenza e grazia: la coltura del cuore*, Collana di testi patristici, 102 (Rome: Città Nuova, 1992), 134–69.

S. Chialà, trans., *Abitare la solitudine*, Testi dei Padri della Chiesa, 72 (Magnano, Monastero di Bose: Edizioni Qiqajon, 2004).

A. Louf, trans., 'Discours sur la cellule', *Collectanea Cisterciensia* 64 (2002), 34–55.

D. Miller, trans., 'Selections from the Book of Grace', in *The Ascetical Homilies of Saint Isaac the Syrian* (Boston: The Holy Transfiguration Monastery, 1984; rev. 2nd edn. 2011), Appendix B.

A. Mingana, trans., *Shem`on the Graceful, Medico-Mystical Work*, Early Christian Mystics, Woodbrooke Studies, 7 (Cambridge: Heffer and Sons, 1934), 1–69.

Theodore of Mopsuestia

A. Mingana, trans., *Commentary of Theodore of Mopsuestia on the Nicene Creed*, Early Christian Mystics, Woodbrooke Studies, 5 (Cambridge: Heffer and Sons, 1932).

MODERN WORKS

H. Alfeyev, *The Spiritual World of Isaac the Syrian*, Cistercian Studies Series, 175 (Kalamazoo: Cistercian Publications, 2000).

—— ed., *St. Isaac the Syrian and His Spiritual Legacy* (New York: St Vladimir's Seminary Press, 2015).

A. H. Becker, *Fear of God and the Beginning of Wisdom: The School of Nisibis and the Development of Scholastic Culture in Late Antique Mesopotamia*, Divinations: Rereading Late Ancient Religion (Philadelphia: University of Pennsylvania Press, 2006).

S. J. Beggiani, 'The Incarnational Theology and Spirituality of John the Solitary of Apamea', *Hugoye: Journal of Syriac Studies* 21/2 (2018), 391–491.

P. Bettiolo, 'Esegesi e purezza di cuore. La testimonianza di Dadišo Qatraya (VII sec.), nestoriano e solitario', *Annali di Storia dell' Esegesi* 3 (1986), 201–13.

——, 'Povertà e Conoscenza. Appunti sulle centurie gnostiche della tradizione evagriana in Siria', *Parole de l'Orient* 15 (1988–9), 107–25.

——, 'Révelations et visions dans l'oeuvre d'Isaac de Ninive: le cadre d'école d'un enseignement spirituel', in *Les Mystiques Syriaques*, ed. by A. Desreumaux, Études Syriaques, 8 (Paris: Geuthner, 2011), 99–119.

R. Beulay, 'L'amour mystique du prochain chez les Syro-Orientaux', in *Patrimoine Syriaque, actes du Colloque VIII* (Antélias: Centre d'Etudes et de Recherches Orientales, 2003), 185–93.

——, *L'enseignement spirituel de Jean de Dalyatha, mystique syro-oriental du VIIIe siècle*, Théologie historique, 83 (Paris: Beauchesne, 1990).

——, *La lumière sans forme. Introduction a l'étude de la mystique chrétienne syro-orientale*, Esprit et Le Feu (Chevetogne: Éditions de Chevetogne, 1987).

B. Bitton-Ashkelony, *The Ladder of Prayer and the Ship of Stirrings* (Leuven: Peeters, 2019), 137–58.

——, 'The Limit of the Mind (NOYΣ): Pure Prayer according to Evagrius Ponticus and Isaac of Nineveh', *Zeitschrift für Antike Christentum/ Journal of Ancient Christianity* 15/2 (2011), 291–321.

——, '"Reduced to a State of Silence": Isaac of Nineveh and John of Dalyatha on Self-transformation' in *St. Isaac the Syrian and his Spiritual Legacy*, ed. by Hilarion Alfeyev (New York: St Vladimir's Seminary Press, 2015), 169–80.

G. G. Blum, 'The Mystology of John the Solitary from Apamea', *The Harp* 5 (1992), 111–29.

S. P. Brock, 'Humanity and the Natural World', *Sobornost incorporating Eastern Churches Review* 12 (1990), 131–42.

——, 'Maggnânûtâ: a Technical Term in East Syrian Spirituality and its Background', in *Mélanges Antoine Guillaumont, contributions à l'étude des christianismes orientaux*, ed. by R.-G. Coquin, Cahiers d'Orientalisme, 20 (Geneva: Patrick Cramer, 1988), 121–9.

——, *Spirituality in the Syriac Tradition*, Mōrān 'Eth'ō, 2 (Kottayam: Saint Ephrem Ecumenical Research Institute, 1989, repr. 2005), 49–59.

——, *The Luminous Eye: The Spiritual World Vision of St. Ephrem* (Kalamazoo: Cistercian Publications, 1992).

——, *The Syriac Fathers on Prayer and the Spiritual Life*, Cistercian Studies Series, 101 (Kalamazoo MI: Cistercian Publications, 1987).

——, 'The Syriac Orient: A Third "Lung" for the Church?', *Orientalia Christiana Periodica* 71/1 (2005), 5–20.

S. Chialà, *Dall' ascesi eremitica alla misericordia infinita. Ricerche su Isacco di Ninive e la sua fortuna*, Biblioteca della Rivista di storia e letteratura religiosa: Studi, 14 (Florence: Leo S. Olschki, 2002).

——, 'Les mystiques Syro-Orientaux: une école ou une époque?', in *Les Mystiques Syriaques*, ed. by A. Desreumaux, Études Syriaques, 8 (Paris: Geuthner, 2011), 63–78.

——, 'L'umiltà nel pensiero di Isacco di Ninive: via di umanizzazione e di divinizzazione', in *Le ricchezze spirituali delle Chiese sire. Atti del 1° Incontro sull'Oriente Cristiano di tradizione siriaca, Milano, Bilblioteca Ambrosiana, 1 marzo 2002*, ed. by E. Vergani and S. Chialà, Ecumenismo e dialogo (Milan: Centro Ambrosiano, 2003), 105–120.

——, 'Simeone di Taibuteh e il suo insegnamento sulla vita nella cella', in *La grande stagione della mistica siro-orientale (VI-VIII secolo). Atti del 5° Incontro sull'Oriente cristiano di tradizione siriaca, Milano, Biblioteca ambrosiana, 26 maggio 2006*, ed. by E. Vergani and S. Chialà, Ecumenismo e dialogo (Centro Ambrosiano, 2010), 121–38.

G. Furlani, 'La psicologia di Aḥûdhemmêh', *Atti della Reale Accademia delle Scienze di Torino: classe di scienze morali, Storiche e Filologiche* 61 (1926), 807–45.

Paulos Mar Gregorios, *The Human Presence: Ecological Spirituality and the Age of the Spirit* (New York: Amity House, 1987).

S. H. Griffith, *Mar Jacob of Serugh on Monks and Monasticism. Readings in his Metrical Homilies 'On the Singles'*, Analecta Gorgiana, 1045 (Piscataway: Gorgias Press, 2011).

——, 'Mar Jacob of Serugh on Monks and Monasticism: Readings in his Metrical Homilies "On the singles"' in *Jacob of Serug and His Times, Studies in Sixth-Century Syriac Christianity*, ed. by G. A. Kiraz, Gorgias Eastern Christian Studies, 8 (Piscataway: Gorgias Press, 2010), 71–89.

——, '"Singles" in God's Service; Thoughts on the Ihidaye from the Works of Aphrahat and Ephraem the Syrian', *The Harp* 4 (1991), 145–59.

——, 'The Image of the Image Maker in the Poetry of St. Ephrem the Syrian', *Studia Patristica* 23 (1993), 258–69.

M. T. Hansbury, '"Insight without Sight": Wonder as an Aspect of Revelation in the Discourses of Isaac the Syrian', *Journal of the Canadian Society for Syriac Studies* 8 (2008), 60–73.

——, 'Remembrance of God and its Relation to Scripture in Isaac III, including Insights from Islamic and Jewish Traditions', in *The Syriac Writers of Qatar in the Seventh Century*, ed. by M. Kozah, A. Abu-Hasayn, S. Al-Murikhi, H. Al-Thani, Gorgias Eastern Christian Studies, 38 (Piscataway: Gorgias Press, 2014), 93–121.

——, 'The Concept of Faith in Isaac the Syrian in the Context of Early Syriac Theology', *Festschrift Rev. Dr. Thomas Koonammakkal, The Harp* 34 (2020), 339–64.

——, 'The Path of Joy in Isaac the Syrian', *Symposium Syriacum XII, Rome, 2016* (Louvain: Peeters, 2020).

C. A. Karim, *Symbols of the Cross in the Writings of the Early Syriac Fathers* (Piscataway: Gorgias Press, 2004).

N. Kavvadas, 'Theodore of Mopsuestia as a Source of Isaac of Nineveh's Pneumatology', *Parole de l'Orient* 35 (2010), 393–405.

G. Kessel, 'La position de Simon de Taibuteh dans l'éventail de la tradition mystique syriaque', in *Les Mystiques Syriaques*, ed. by A. Desreumaux, Études Syriaques, 8 (Paris: Geuthner, 2011), 121–50.

——, 'The Activity of Grace in the "Book of Grace". Some Preliminary Observations', in *Christliche Gotteslehre im Orient seit dem Anfkommen des Islams bis zur Gegenwart*, ed. by M. Tamcke, Beiruter Texte und Studien, 126 (Beirut/Wurzburg: Ergon Verlag, 2008), 57–68.

N. Khayyat, 'Le Visage du Christ resplendissant dans le miroir du coeur', in *Le Visage de Dieu dans le Patrimoine Oriental, Patrimoine Syriaque, actes de colloque VII* (Antélias: Centre d'Études et de Recherches Orientales, 2001), 77–87.

G. A. Kiraz, ed., *Jacob of Serug and his Times: Studies in Sixth-Century Syriac Christianity*, Gorgias Eastern Christian Studies, 8 (Piscataway: Gorgias Press, 2010).

J. Kollaparambil, 'Cross and Crucifix in the Syrian Tradition', *The Harp* 8–9 (1995–6), 77–183.

K.-H. Kuhlmann, 'Healing in St. Ephrem's Commentary on Diatessaron', *The Harp* 4 (1991), 35–47.

J. M. Lera, 'Theodore of Mopsuestia', *Dictionnaire de spiritualité ascétique et mystique: doctrine et histoire* 17 vols (Paris: G. Beauchesne et ses fils, 1932–1995) xv, 385–400.

F. G. McLeod, *The Roles of Christ's Humanity in Salvation: Insights from Theodore of Mopsuestia* (Washington DC: Catholic University of America Press, 2005).

R. Murray, *The Cosmic Covenant: Biblical Themes of Justice, Peace and the Integrity of Creation* (London: Sheed & Ward, 1992).

M. Nin, 'La "Lettera sulle tre tappe della vita monastica" di Giuseppe Hazzaya' in *Il monachesimo tra eredità e aperture. Atti del simposio "Testi e Temi nella Tradizione del Monachesimo Cristiano" per il 50° anniversario dell'Istituto Monastico di Sant'Anselmo; Roma, 28 maggio – 1° giugno 2002*, ed. by M. Bielawski and D. Hombergen, Studia Anselmiana, 140/Analecta Monastica, 8 (Roma: Pontificio Ateneo S. Anselmo, 2004), 307–22.

——, 'La sintesi monastica di Giovanni il Solitario' in *Le Chiese sire tra IV e VI secolo: dibattito dottrinale e ricerca spirituale. Atti del 2° Incontro sull'Oriente Cristiano di tradizione siriaca, Milano, Biblioteca Ambrosiana, 28 marzo 2003*, ed. by E. Vergani and S. Chialà, Ecumenismo e Dialogo (Milan: Centro Ambrosiano, 2005), 95–117.

——, 'Martyrius/Sahdona: alcuni aspetti del suo insegnamento cristologico', in *La grande stagione della mistica siro-orientale (VI-VIII secolo). Atti del 5° Incontro sull'Oriente cristiano di tradizione siriaca, Milano, Biblioteca ambrosiana, 26 maggio 2006*, ed. by E. Vergani and S. Chialà, Ecumenismo e Dialogo (Milan: Centro Ambrosiano, 2009), 29–69.

I. Ovidiu, 'Martyrius-Sahdona: la pensée christologique, clé de la théologie mystique', in *Les Mystiques Syriaques*, ed. by A. Desreumaux, Études Syriaques, 8 (Paris: Geuthner, 2011), 61–87.

C. Pasquet, 'L'homme, lien de l'univers, dans la tradition syro-orientale', *Studia Patristica* 45 (2010), 203–10.

F. del Río Sánchez, 'Dadišho' du Qatar et la quietude', in *Les Mystiques Syriaques*, ed. by A. Desreumaux, Etudes Syriaques, 8 (Paris: Geuthner, 2011), 87–98.

Mor A. Y. Samuel, ed., *M'ade'dono: The Book of the Church Festivals According to the Ancient Rite of the Syrian Orthodox Church of Antioch*, trans. by M. Barsom (Piscataway: Gorgias Press, 2011).

G. G. Scholem, *Major Trends in Jewish Mysticism* (New York: Schocken Books, 1941).

D. L. Schwartz, *Paideia and Cult. Christian Initiation in Theodore of Mopsuestia*, Hellenic Studies, 57 (Cambridge MA: Harvard University Press, 2013).

J. Scully, *Isaac of Nineveh's Ascetical Eschatology*, Oxford Early Christian Studies (Oxford: Oxford University Press, 2017).

——, 'The Transmission of Evagrian Theological Concepts into East Syrian Christianity: A Comparison of Evagrius and Sahdona on Contemplation and Anthropology', *Greek Orthodox Theological Review* 54/1–4 (2009), 77–96.

S. Seppälä, 'Angelic mysticism in John of Dalyatha', *Parole de l'Orient* 41 (2015), 425–33.

——, 'Angelology of St. Isaac the Syrian', in *St. Isaac the Syrian and his Spiritual Legacy: Proceedings of the International Patristics Conference, Moscow, 2013*, ed. by H. Alfeyev (New York: St Vladimir's Seminary Press, 2015), 97–113.

——, 'The Holy Spirit in Isaac of Nineveh and East Syrian Mysticism', in *The Holy Spirit in the Fathers of the Church: Proceedings of the Seventh International Patristics Conference, Maynooth, 2008*, ed. by D. W. Twomey, J. E. Rutherford (Dublin: Four Courts Press, 2010), 127–50.

A. Shemunkasho, *Healing in the Theology of Saint Ephrem*, Gorgias Studies in Early Christianity and Patristics, 1 (Piscataway: Gorgias Press, repr. 2004).

——, 'Salvation History as a Process of Healing in the Theology of Mor Ephrem', *The Harp* 11–12 (1998–9), 175–86.

——, 'The Healing of Interior and Exterior Blindness in Ephrem', *Studia Patristica* 35 (2001), 494–501.

C. Stewart, 'Imageless Prayer and the Theological Vision of Evagrius Ponticus', *Journal of Early Christian Studies* 9/2 (2001), 173–204.

E. Urbach, *The Sages: Their Concepts and Beliefs*, Publications of the Perry Foundation in the Hebrew University of Jerusalem (Jerusalem: Magnes Press, 1979).

V. Vesa, *Knowledge and Experience in the Writings of St. Isaac of Nineveh*, Gorgias Eastern Christian Studies, 51 (Piscataway, NJ: Gorgias Press 2018).

M. Zonta, 'Nemesiana Syriaca: New Fragments from the Missing Syriac Version of the *De Natura Hominis*', *Journal of Semitic Studies* 36/2 (1991), 223–58.

PATRISTICS TEXTS PUBLISHED BY SLG PRESS

Available from www.slgpress.co.uk

FP048   *The Wisdom of the Desert Fathers*
trans. Sr Benedicta Ward SLG (1975)   £8.00

FP050   *Letters of Saint Antony the Great*
trans. Derwas Chitty (1975)   £5.00

FP072   *The Letters of Ammonas, Successor of St Antony*
trans. Derwas Chitty (1979)   £2.00

FP094   *Saint Gregory Nazianzen: Selected Poem*
trans. John McGuckin (1986)   £2.25

FP095   *The World of the Desert Fathers: Stories & Sayings from the Anonymous Series of the 'Apophthegmata Patrum'*
trans. Columba Stewart OSB (1986)   £3.50

FP128   *The Wisdom of Saint Isaac the Syrian*
Sebastian Brock (1997)   £5.00

FP145   *The Reflections of Abba Zosimas, Monk of the Palestinian Desert*
trans. John Chryssavgis (2004)   £5.00

FP149   *Hymns of Saint Ephrem the Syrian*
trans. Mary Hansbury (2006)   £5.50

FP171   *The Spiritual Wisdom of the Syriac Book of Steps*
Robert A Kitchen (2013)   £5.50

FP173   *On Tour in Byzantium: Excerpts from The Spiritual Meadow of John Moschus*
Ralph Martin SSM (2013)   £7.00

FP177   *The Prayers of Jacob of Serugh*
ed. Mary Hansbury (2015)   £8.00

FP179   *The Desert of the Heart: Daily Readings with the Desert Fathers*
trans. Sr Benedicta Ward SLG (2016)   £6.50

FP001	*Prayer and the Life of Reconciliation*	Gilbert Shaw (1969)	£0.50
FP002	*Aloneness Not Loneliness*	Mother Mary Clare SLG (1969)	£0.50
FP004	*Intercession*	Mother Mary Clare SLG (1969)	£0.40
FP008	*Prayer: Extracts from the Teaching of Fr Gilbert Shaw*	Gilbert Shaw (1973)	£1.00
FP012	*Learning to Pray*	Mother Mary Clare SLG (1970)	£2.50
FP015	*Death, the Gateway to Life*	Gilbert Shaw (1971)	£1.25
FP016	*The Victory of the Cross*	Dumitru Stăniloae (1970)	£5.00
FP026	*The Message of Saint Seraphim*	Irina Gorainov (1974)	£5.00
FP028	*Julian of Norwich: 4 Studies to Commemorate the 6th Centenary of the Revelations of Divine Love* ed. A. M. Allchin	Sr Benedicta Ward SLG, Sr Eileen Mary SLG (1973)	£6.50
FP043	*The Power of the Name: The Jesus Prayer in Orthodox Spirituality*	Kallistos Ware (1974)	£6.00
FP046	*Prayer and Contemplation and Distractions are for Healing*	Robert Llewelyn (1975)	£5.95
FP048	*The Wisdom of the Desert Fathers*	trans. Sr Benedicta Ward SLG (1975)	£8.00
FP050	*Letters of Saint Antony the Great*	trans. Derwas Chitty (1975)	£5.00
FP054	*From Loneliness to Solitude*	Roland Walls (1976)	£1.00
FP055	*Theology and Spirituality*	Andrew Louth (1976)	£2.00
FP061	*Kabir: The Way of Love and Paradox*	Sr Rosemary SLG (1977)	£2.50
FP062	*Anselm of Canterbury: A Monastic Scholar*	Sr Benedicta Ward SLG (1973)	£4.00
FP067	*Mary and the Mystery of the Incarnation: An Essay on the Mother of God in the Theology of Karl Barth*	Andrew Louth (1977)	£4.00
FP068	*Trinity and Incarnation in Anglican Tradition*	A. M. Allchin (1977)	£1.25
FP070	*Facing Depression*	Gonville ffrench-Beytagh (1978)	£1.00
FP071	*The Single Person*	Philip Welsh (1979)	£1.00
FP072	*The Letters of Ammonas, Successor of St Antony*	trans. Derwas Chitty (1979)	£2.00
FP074	*George Herbert, Priest and Poet*	Kenneth Mason (1980)	£2.50
FP075	*A Study of Wisdom: Three Tracts by the Author of The Cloud of Unknowing*	(1980)	£9.00
FP078	*Silence in Prayer and Action*	Sr Edmée SLG (1981)	£1.50
FP081	*The Psalms: Prayer Book of the Bible*	Dietrich Bonhoeffer, trans. Sr Isabel SLG (1982)	£5.00
FP082	*Prayer and Holiness*	Dumitru Stăniloae (1982)	£6.50
FP085	*Eight Chapters on Perfection and Angels' Song*	Walter Hilton, trans. Rosemary Dorward (1983)	£1.50

FP133   *Love Unknown: Meditations on the Death and Resurrection of Jesus*
                                John Barton (1999)   £3.50
FP134   *The Hidden Way of Love: Jean-Pierre de Caussade's Spirituality*
        of Abandonment   Barry Conaway (1999)   £3.00
FP135   *Shepherd and Servant: The Spiritual Theology of Saint Dunstan*
                                Douglas Dales (2000)   £2.50
FP136   *Eternity and Time*
                        Dumitru Stăniloae, trans. A. M. Allchin (2001)   £2.00
FP137   *Pilgrimage of the Heart*   Sr Benedicta Ward SLG (2001)   £2.25
FP138   *Mixed Life*   Walter Hilton, trans. Rosemary Dorward (2001)   £3.00
FP140   *A Great Joy: Reflections on the Meaning of Christmas*
                                Kenneth Mason (2001)   £2.50
FP141   *Bede and the Psalter*   Sr Benedicta Ward SLG (2002)   £3.00
FP142   *Abhishiktananda: A Memoir of Dom Henri Le Saux (Abhishiktananda)*
                        Murray Rogers, David Barton (2003)   £4.50
FP143   *Friendship in God: The Encounter of Evelyn Underhill & Sorella*
        Maria of Campello   A. M. Allchin (2003)   £3.00
FP144   *Christian Imagination in Poetry and Polity: Some Anglican Voices*
        from Temple to Herbert.   Archbishop Rowan Williams (2004)   £4.00
FP145   *The Reflections of Abba Zosimas, Monk of the Palestinian Desert*
                                trans. John Chryssavgis (2004)   £5.00
FP146   *The Gift of Theology: The Trinitarian Vision of Ann Griffiths and*
        Elizabeth of Dijon   A. M. Allchin (2005)   £3.00
FP147   *Sacrifice and Spirit*   Bishop Michael Ramsey (2005)   £2.00
FP148   *Saint John Cassian on Prayer*   trans. A. M Casiday (2006)   £6.50
FP149   *Hymns of Saint Ephrem the Syrian*
                                trans. Mary Hansbury (2006)   £5.50
FP150   *Suffering: Why all this suffering? What do I do about it?*
                Reinhard Körner OCD, trans. Sr Avis Mary SLG (2006)   £3.00
FP151   *A True Easter: The Synod of Whitby 664 AD*
                                Sr Benedicta Ward SLG (2007)   £5.00
FP152   *Prayer as Self-offering*   Alexander Ryrie (2007)   £1.50
FP153   *From Perfection to the Elixir: How George Herbert Fashioned*
        a Famous Poem   Ben de la Mare (2008)   £3.00
FP154   *The Jesus Prayer: Gospel Soundings*
                                Sr Pauline Margaret CHN (2008)   £3.50
FP155   *Loving God Whatever: Through the Year with Sister Jane*
                                Sister Jane SLG (2006)   £9.00
FP156   *Prayer and Meditation for a Sleepless Night*   (1993)   £0.50
FP157   *Being There: Caring for the Bereaved*   John Porter (2009)   £3.50
FP158   *Learn to Be at Peace: The Practice of Stillness*
                                Andrew Norman (2010)   £2.00
FP159   *From Holy Week to Easter*   George Pattison (2010)   £4.00

www.slgpress.co.uk